Lessons for the Urban Century

Lessons for the Urban Century

Decentralized Infrastructure Finance in the World Bank

Patricia Clarke Annez
Gwénaelle Huet
George E. Peterson

 THE WORLD BANK

ISBN-13: 978-0-8213-7524-2
eISBN: 978-0-8213-7525-9
DOI: 10.1596/978-0-8213-7524-2

Library of Congress Cataloging-in-Publication Data

Annez, Patricia Clarke.
  Lessons for the urban century: decentralized infrastructure finance in the World Bank / Patricia Clarke Annez, Gwénaelle Huet, and George E. Peterson.
     p. cm.
  Includes bibliographical references and index.
  ISBN 978-0-8213-7524-2 — ISBN 978-0-8213-7525-9 (electronic)
1. Municipal finance—Developing countries. 2.Infrastructure (Economics)—Developing countries—Finance. 3. World Bank. I. Huet, Gwénaelle. II. Peterson, George E. III. Title.
  HJ9695.A56 2008
  332.1'532—dc22

                        2008016697

Cover design: Naylor Design, Washington DC, United States

Contents

Foreword		*ix*
Acknowledgments		*xi*
About the Authors		*xiii*
Abbreviations and Acronyms		*xv*
Executive Summary		*xix*
Chapter 1	**Introduction and Objective**	1
	The Role of Demographics	2
	The Role of Decentralization	5
	The Role of Financial Liberalization	6
	Objective of this Review of Experience	7
Chapter 2	**Trends and Structure of Urban Infrastructure Funds (UIFs)**	9
	Composition of UIFs by Sector Board over Time	10
	Long-Term Trends in the Volume of UIF Lending	11
Chapter 3	**Performance of UIFs**	17
Chapter 4	**UIF Design: Options for Intermediation Strategy**	21

Chapter 5   Learning from Experience in Project Design   31
              Transplanting the Line of Credit Model
                  in Sub-Saharan Africa   31
              South Asia: Adapting the Credit Model   36
              Rethinking Support for Local Infrastructure
                  Investment: Municipal Grants and Social Funds   37
              Supporting Municipal Infrastructure Investment
                  in Centralized Systems   43
              Commercial Banks and the Development
                  of Sustainable Municipal Credit Systems   46

Chapter 6   Agenda for Future Work   51

Chapter 7   Conclusions   63

Appendix 1   Methodology for Selecting and
              Identifying Urban Infrastructure
              Funds Financed by the World Bank   69

Appendix 2   List of UIFs Reviewed   75

Appendix 3   List of Currencies Available for Swaps
              from IBRD Loans as of January 3, 2008   83

References   85
Index   89

Boxes

4.1   A Model of Market-Oriented Reform:
       Crédit Local de France   24
6.1   Monitoring Municipal Financial Market
       Development: The Czech Republic   58

Figures

1.1.   Urban versus Rural Population Growth Worldwide
       through 2030   3
1.2.   World Urban Population Growth through 2030:
       Low- and Middle-Income versus High-Income Countries   3

1.3.   Distribution of World Urban Population Growth
       through 2015 by City Size   4
1.4.   Selected Mega Cities' Growth Rates through 2010   5
2.1.   UIF Commitments by Region and Sector Board   10
2.2.   UIF Commitments by Country   10
2.3.   Annual UIF Commitments by Sector Board   11
2.4.   Trends in Total Urban Infrastructure Fund Lending—
       Annual Averages   11
2.5.   Trends in Annual Average Urban Infrastructure Fund
       Lending by Infrastructure and Non-infrastructure
       Sector Boards   12
2.6.   Trends in Annual Average Project Size   13
2.7.   UIF Lending Projects   14
2.8.   UIF Grant Projects   14
3.1.   Outcome Ratings for UIFs   18
3.2.   Selected Outcome Ratings for UIFs by Sector Board   18
3.3.   Disbursements as a Percentage of Commitments for UIFs   19
3.4.   Loan Recoveries in UIFs: Reporting and Repayment
       Rates by Institutional Arrangement   20
4.1.   Loan Financing versus Grant Financing
       of Subprojects by Sector Board   27
4.2.   Development Objective: Development
       of Municipal Credit Market by Sector Board   28
4.3.   Development Objective: Development of Municipal
       Credit Market over Time   28
A1.1. World Bank Project Approvals: FY1971–FY2006   70

Tables

1.1.   UIFs by Region   7
4.1.   Financial Intermediation versus Poverty-Oriented Grants   27
5.1.   Municipal On-Lending Projects in Sub-Saharan Africa   33
5.2.   Municipal Grants and Infrastructure Programs   40
A1.1. UIF Projects by Region   72

Foreword

The world recently passed a significant threshold: it is now more urban than rural. Over the next 30 years, most world population growth will be in cities in developing countries. Among these urban areas, most of the growth will be concentrated in smaller cities. Highly visible mega cities will continue to grow, but more slowly on the whole, while cities with fewer than 1 million in population are projected to absorb an increase of nearly one half billion in the next 15 years.

These demographic changes will give rise to unprecedented demands for investments in infrastructure in thousands of cities and towns. Given the simultaneous move toward the decentralization of fiscal responsibilities, the weak financial and technical capacity of local governments will become an increasingly serious constraint. Providing the services to keep these cities livable will be a major challenge for developing countries and for international development agencies seeking to support that endeavor. Reaching large numbers of municipalities with relatively small investment needs will become a critical function of development programs.

This book provides insights into how best to meet that challenge, based on evidence from the World Bank's operations supporting decentralized urban infrastructure finance over nearly 30 years around the world. From this varied and rich set of experiences emerge lessons learned, suggestions for the future, and an agenda for future work.

The distinctive feature of decentralized urban infrastructure finance projects is the use of domestic institutions to identify, appraise, and channel financing to subnational entities (municipalities, local utilities, and community groups) on behalf of the World Bank. This feature is critical to moving beyond mega cities and major capitals and reaching large numbers of small municipalities. Not only external financiers but also central governments must learn to design institutions that can perform this role if they are to operate cost-effectively and meet the needs of their growing urban populations. This capacity is fundamental to "scaling up" beyond small pilot projects to programs that improve urban services nationwide.

This is the first study that reviews these projects as a group. Some of the results are quite encouraging. These operations, more than 100 separate World Bank projects that date from the 1970s, account for $11 billion in infrastructure finance. Together these projects have performed better than the average for the World Bank. A variety of successful designs have been tried and adapted in a host of contexts. Less encouraging is the decline in this type of lending since the mid-1990s, particularly puzzling considering it occurred just as decentralization and democratization were becoming widespread in the developing world.

The World Bank is committed to reinvigorating this line of business as part of the Sustainable Infrastructure Action Plan. Doing so will mean addressing the reasons for the decline in this type of lending, partnering with our clients to understand their evolving needs, and adapting this versatile product accordingly.

The single most important lesson learned from this review of experience is that any successful model requires careful tailoring to reflect the specific needs of local governments, the state of intergovernmental relations, financial sector development, and the political economic forces at play in local and central government. In the World Bank, we welcome this challenge to expand our reach while offering products that are customized to meet our clients' needs to build more livable and sustainable cities.

Katherine Sierra
Vice President
Sustainable Development Network
The World Bank

Acknowledgments

The authors would like to thank Robert Buckley, Catherine Farvacque, Mila Freire, Roy Gilbert, Sonia Hammam, Lawrence Hannah, Kamran Khan, Thierry Paulais (Agence Française de Développement), and Hiroaki Suzuki, as well as participants in seminars and review meetings in the World Bank, who provided very helpful comments on this work. The authors are most grateful to Johannes Linn (Brookings Institution), Ken Davey (University of Birmingham), Christine Kessides (World Bank), and Krishnaswamy Rajivan (Cities Alliance), who served as peer reviewers and offered many useful insights and suggestions for improvement.

Special thanks are owed to Xaiofeng Li and Berenice Sanchez for their help in preparing the manuscript for publication; to Laura de Brular and Christianna Johnnides for their generous and willing assistance in using internal databases, to Patricia Katayama, Elizabeth Kline, and Cathy Lips for their help and encouragement during the editorial process, and to Jerry Kalarickal and Ashna Mathema for their valuable input to the empirical analysis for the book. The authors would also like to thank the École Nationale des Ponts et Chaussées (France) for its support for Gwénaelle Huet's internship at the World Bank to contribute to this work. The book was prepared under the general supervision of Mila Freire, Abha Joshi-Ghani, and Laszlo Lovei.

About the Authors

Patricia Clarke Annez is the Urban Advisor in the Finance Economics and Urban Department. She has worked in the World Bank's Operations and Finance departments as well as the Research and Policy section, and has operational experience in several regions. As chief of the Urban Division, she managed the World Bank's contributions to the Habitat II Conference in Istanbul in 1996. Ms. Annez is the head of the Urban Economics, Finance and Management Thematic Group. She has also worked as an economic and financial advisor for ABB in Canada and for U.S. corporate clients in New York. She recently published *Financing Cities: Fiscal Responsibility and Urban Infrastructure in Brazil, China, India, South Africa and Poland* (Sage: 2007), co-edited with George E. Peterson, and *Urbanization and Growth*, co-edited with A. Michael Spence and Robert Buckley (Forthcoming: World Bank).

Gwénaelle Huet worked on this review during an internship in the Urban Development unit of the World Bank for her master's degree in public policy from the *Ecole Nationale des Ponts et Chaussées*. She also earned a master's degrees in physics (*Ecole Normale Supérieure*) and passed the *Agrégation* in physics. She has worked with the *St. Gobain* Group in Worcester, Massachusetts on commercialization of renewable energy, and with the French Atomic Energy Commission on nuclear energy. She is currently working for the Service of the Prime Minister in France within the General Secretary for European Affairs, with responsibility for energy and competitiveness matters.

George E. Peterson is a consultant to the World Bank and other international organizations on public finance and urban infrastructure. He was Senior Fellow in International Public Finance at the Urban Institute for ten years, and prior to that Director of the Public Finance Center of the Urban Institute. Recent publications include *Financing Cities: Fiscal Responsibility and Urban Infrastructure in Brazil, China, India, Poland, and South Africa* (co-editor with Patricia Clarke Annez: Sage 2007), *Decentralization in Asia and Latin America* (co-editor: Edward Elgar 2006), and *Land-Based Financing of Urban Infrastructure* (forthcoming with Paul Smoke and Eduardo J. Gómez, World Bank). He is the author of *Building Local Credit Systems* (World Bank).

Abbreviations and Acronyms

Note: Unless otherwise specified, dollars $ refers to US dollars.

AFD	Agence Française de Développement
AFR	Africa Region, World Bank
AGETIP	Agence d'Exécution de Travaux d'Intérêt Public
APL	Adaptable Program Loan
BP	Bank Procedure, World Bank
BW	Business Warehouse
CLF	Credit Local de France
CPSCL	Caisse de Prêts et de Soutien aux Collectivités Locales
DPL	Development Policy Loan
EAP	East Asia and the Pacific Region, World Bank
ECA	Europe and Central Asia Region, World Bank
EIB	European Investment Bank
EMT	Energy and Mining
ENV	Environment
EP	Economic Policy
ERL	Emergency Recovery Loan
ERR	economic rate of return
EU	European Union

FEC   Fonds d'Equipement Communal
FIL   Financial Intermediary Loan
FINDETER   Financiera de Desarrollo Territorial Sociedad Anonyma
FS   Financial Sector
FY   fiscal year
GDP   gross domestic product
GIC   Global Information and Communications
IADB   Inter-American Development Bank
IAP   Infrastructure Action Plan
IBRD   International Bank for Reconstruction and
             Development
ICR   Implementation Completion Report
IDA   International Development Association
IEG   Independent Evaluation Group
IFC   International Finance Corporation
IFI   international financial institution
IPO   initial public offering
Kc   Czech crown (koruna)
LAC   Latin America and the Caribbean Region, World Bank
LDC   less developed country
LIL   Learning and Innovation Loan
LOC   line of credit
MAP   Municipal Adjustment Plan
MIC   Middle Income Countries
MIGA   Multilateral Investment Guarantee Agency
MDF   municipal development fund
MNA   Middle East and North Africa Region, World Bank
MoF   Ministry of Finance
MUFIS   Municipal Infrastructure Finance Company
NGO   nongovernmental organization
OD   Operational Directive
OED   Operations Evaluation Department
OP   Operational Policy
PAD   Project Appraisal Document
PMU   Project Management Unit
PO   Poverty Reduction
PPP   Public-Private Partnership
PREM   Poverty Reduction and Economic Management
PRSC   Poverty Reduction Support Credit

PS	Public Sector
PSD	Private Sector Development
RDV	Rural Development
SAD	Sector Adjustment Loan
SAL	Structural Adjustment Loan
SAR	South Asia Region, World Bank
SDV	Social Development
SF	Social Fund
SIL	Specific Investment Loan
SIM	Sector Investment and Maintenance Loan
SP	Social Protection
SSA	Sub-Saharan Africa
SSL	Special Structural Adjustment Loan
TAL	Technical Assistance Loan
TNUDF	Tamil Nadu Urban Development Fund
TR	Transport
UD	Urban Development
UDDP	Urban Development and Decentralization Project
UIF	urban infrastructure fund
UN	United Nations
USAID	United States Agency for International Development
WB	World Bank
WSS	Water Supply and Sanitation

Executive Summary

This book takes a look at the past to gain insights for the future. Nearly 30 years ago, when the world urban population was only about half of the 3 billion that it is today, when most less developed countries (LDCs) were primarily rural, and before the wave of decentralization of the 1980s and 1990s, the World Bank developed an instrument with great potential. The key characteristics of this instrument, the urban infrastructure fund (UIF), are several.[1] It provides finance for an array of urban services, not just one sector, such as water and sanitation, leaving flexibility for local beneficiaries to set their priorities. UIF projects operate in more than one city. Perhaps the most important distinctive feature is that these projects use local institutions to do the work of identifying, appraising and channeling finance to subnational entities (municipalities, local utilities, or community groups) on behalf of the World Bank.[2] This arrangement

---

[1]Urban infrastructure funds are also commonly referred to as municipal development funds (MDFs). However, some of the projects with the characteristics we are seeking not only targeted municipalities as beneficiaries, but also included local community groups or nongovernmental organizations (NGOs), for example, as sponsors of local infrastructure projects. For this reason, we used the less common, but more comprehensive, terminology.

[2]The scope of the empirical work in this book is limited to World Bank projects, and hence we draw conclusions with reference to the World Bank. This limitation of scope in no sense implies a judgment as to the relevance of these conclusions or lack thereof for other international institutions. That is a subject that should be explored; the World Bank and other international financial institutions (IFIs) could benefit from pooling their experience.

makes it feasible to reach beyond the major capitals or business centers such as Chongqing, Mumbai, or São Paulo, or even regional capitals, to fund much smaller subprojects, suited to the needs and capacities of smaller cities and towns, because local agents are tasked with identifying and appraising these projects.

Delegating these functions makes it practicable not only for a large international financial institution (IFI) such as the World Bank but also for national governments to reach small municipalities. Providing support to large numbers of municipalities with relatively small investment needs is a complex task, but it is fundamental to scaling up beyond small pilot projects to programs improving urban services countrywide.

Demographic and Operational Trends

Enhancing this capacity to reach secondary cities and towns is important for the World Bank's future, first and foremost because of demographics. In the last year, an important threshold was passed; half of the world's population is now urban. More than 80 percent of future expansion of urban population in developing countries is expected to take place in cities with populations less than 5 million, more than 50 percent in cities with less than 1 million. This development will give rise to huge demands for new urban infrastructure outside of the principal cities. For the World Bank, developing instruments that expand its operational reach to meet these needs is central to its impact and relevance for the development agenda in the 21st century—the first urban century.

Pioneered in the late 1970s, urban infrastructure fund projects account for World Bank commitments of about US$11 billion in constant 2006 dollars. The UIF has been a successful line of business. Overall the rate of fully or highly satisfactory projects[3] is higher than the World Bank average, and performance in comparison to World Bank lines of credit (LOCs) in general is considerably better. Loan recovery rates and disbursement rates are better than in other World Bank lines of credit and in public banks more generally. UIF projects used community participation and sought to build access to private participation early on, before these approaches were mainstreamed in the World Bank.

It is thus puzzling that, after a rapid growth for the first 15 years, use of this instrument stagnated and then declined. Annual average lending

---

[3]Rated by the Independent Evaluation Group (IEG), formerly the Operations Evaluation Department (OED), as "highly satisfactory" or "satisfactory." To focus on performance that is "fully satisfactory" or better, this study excluded the "marginally satisfactory" category.

in real terms for UIFs in 2004–06, the first three years of the Infrastructure Action Plan (IAP), was about US$360 million. This is less than 70 percent of the peak value reached more than a decade ago, in FY1989–93 (US$525 million). The decline in lending for UIFs cannot be explained simply by the decline of infrastructure lending overall, or as a result of the difficulties in lending to middle-income countries (MICs). In fact, the share of UIFs in the Urban Development (UD) sector board's portfolio declined during FY1994–FY2006 in the International Bank for Reconstruction and Development (IBRD) and the International Development Association (IDA) operations alike. These factors have doubtless played some role, but it also appears that this decline is related to the overall reduction in lines of credit subsequent to the Levy report,[4] published in 1989.

This book argues that the trend should be reversed and uses lessons of experience to demonstrate that the World Bank has the knowledge and tools to do so effectively if it can muster the flexibility to adapt the UIF product to meet emerging client needs.

Lessons from UIF Experience

A critical step in the process of rebuilding and renewing this line of business is recognizing that the World Bank has already developed widely varying intermediation models, with distinct strengths and weaknesses in different situations. These models lie on a continuum between two extremes: direct private market access and poverty-oriented grant funds. Tailoring the intermediation model to work in a specific-country context for specific investment needs is essential to designing a successful UIF.

It is interesting that just as the volume of lending declined in the mid-1990s, so too was there a decline in operations occupying the middle ground on this continuum, evidence of a disinclination to use the flexibility inherent in the UIF model. In the latter part of the 1990s, the UIF projects that were approved tended to be at the extreme ends of the spectrum: either small social fund–type grant projects or projects providing loans to local governments with ambitious objectives for private sector involvement.

Experience from that period shows that this more rigid and extreme vision of a good UIF project runs not only the risk of taking the World Bank out of the business (which it clearly has), but it does not necessarily

---

[4] *Report of the Task Force on Financial Sector Operations*, R98-163. World Bank, August 1, 1989.

improve results on the ground. The ambitious reform objectives often had to be rethought and detracted attention from solid yet gradual improvements. Although the poverty-oriented grant funds were clearly useful tools, especially in countries in distress, eventually it came to be recognized that these operations could not substitute fully for projects that sponsored larger investments and worked directly with municipalities.

This book discusses experiences with individual UIF projects that span a range of regions and types of project design. The lessons learned are worth reading in detail for practitioners in the field. Some highlights follow.

Caution and good contextual knowledge are especially important in using the on-lending model. Particularly in poor countries, competing sources of grant funds from other donors are likely to make it hard for a credit line to disburse. Optimistic projections of local government capacity to borrow must also be viewed with a very critical eye. **It is not safe to assume that local governments will increase their revenue streams dramatically simply to be able to take on a loan for new infrastructure, no matter how useful.** Even expert consultants such as rating agencies may overestimate the scope for revenue improvement if a large external project is at stake. A series of unsuccessful early UIFs relying on the lending and private sector model in Sub-Saharan Africa illustrate this problem. Later, the development of more realistic and successful UIFs in Sub-Saharan Africa using primarily grants illustrates the World Bank's capacity to adapt the UIF product and the payoffs of doing so.

It is very hard to promote a rapid transition to the private market access model for local governments in countries that have experienced limited fiscal and administrative decentralization. Local governments are not viable clients for private lenders until they reach a certain critical threshold of autonomy and fiscal viability. **However, the "decentralization constraint" should not necessarily preclude using UIFs.** There are successful UIF models in India, Morocco, and Tunisia, for example, which have delivered on the promise of helping secondary cities improve their infrastructure more efficiently and effectively than they could have on their own, even if the projects did not promote either rapid decentralization or private credit access. But support of the higher level of government for the credit line and the institutional objectives is critical. Alignment with the current state of play on intergovernmental relations is a key ingredient of a successful fund. Although a UIF operation can support reform in this area, consistent with experience with other types of investment projects, it is typically not the instrument of choice if the primary objective is intergovernmental reform. Dedicated policy loans are a better, complementary instrument for focusing on policy reforms. UIF projects need to focus on investments; however, a successful UIF operation can help build a stakeholder base to support reforms.

Financial deregulation and decentralization have changed the way we need to design UIFs; they have not made the UIF irrelevant. The financial sectors in most of our client countries have changed considerably in the past 20 years. Financial deregulation can bring in new players that may be interested in lending to local governments, provided this can be made a profitable business. At the same time, decentralization proceeds at a pace that has little to do with financial sector developments, so following the latest financial sector trends may not be suited to a good municipal operation. The financial model used in a UIF must be aligned with the state of decentralization and the types of investments the project seeks to support. No matter how dynamic the financial sector, it will not meet the investment needs of all local governments for all investments. Important opportunities are missed by assuming that subsidies for urban investments are no longer needed because the financial sector is more flexible than it once was.

In UIFs, the most typical project design involves establishing a new, specialized institution to work with the World Bank, for example, municipal development funds (MDFs) or social funds. When financial sector reform or decentralization is in an early stage, a dedicated institution or facility is often the only workable model. The alternative of providing a facility to existing institutions, such as commercial banks for on-lending, has been tried, in some cases quite successfully. This was especially true when the financial sector was becoming competitive and there was new entry into different market niches. When such institutions already are lending or are interested in lending to local governments, this is most likely the best approach.

But working with independent institutions that the World Bank has not created requires flexibility, responsiveness, and manageable procedures to make it worth their while to participate in a World Bank project. Likewise, when project design seeks to make a specialized lending institution compete with other institutions, there is a need for parsimony in the special demands made for social targeting and compliance with safeguards. This restraint is needed to ensure that those demands do not detract from the level playing field the World Bank is trying to promote.

It pays to keep project objectives and instruments simple. Although this may seem a platitude, the complexity and overload of corporate objectives of some UIF projects are striking. This tendency was aggravated when concerns about directed credit placed fund operations in a bad light. As one peer reviewer of this book noted, "Retailing credit to a plethora of projects in the back of beyond is complicated enough without trying to satisfy every latest doctrinal whim."[5]

The World Bank has developed workable models for a variety of needs and objectives, and the high average outcome ratings for UIFs attest to this. The many successful projects typically focused on one or two objectives and executed them simply. Less successful projects tried to achieve all of them.

Many projects have encountered difficulties with overambitious plans for municipal borrowing as opposed to grants. UIFs that are not social funds have tended to shy away from grants, in large part because providing subsidies for infrastructure in urban areas is perceived to promote urban bias for relatively well-off urban populations. The Social Fund model tends to specialize in grants provided selectively on the basis of geographical poverty indicators. This is only one among many possible approaches to targeting the government subsidies that are provided by central governments to municipalities. **More UIF projects need to focus on efficient distribution of subsidies, even for infrastructure services in urban areas.** Reliance on credit models before the time is ripe, although appealing at the design stage, can lead to two types of implementation problems: the available funds aren't used fully, or beneficiaries receive subsidies anyway, but they are distributed with little deliberation or transparency.

Much more skepticism of decentralization is needed. Assume decentralization will proceed half as quickly as predicted, then halve that estimate again to come up with a credit market model and institutional development objectives. Some less successful projects chose an inferior model design based on the notion that a government declaration of decentralization or an expressed desire that municipalities fend for themselves was sufficient to make that model work.

Special caution is needed when transplanting models from other countries. Many of the local subtleties of political economy and appetite for decentralization may be overlooked when trying to make a model that was successful elsewhere work in a new environment. Rather than promise more than a fund project can deliver in terms of intergovernmental reform, effective UIF projects plan for incremental improvement of what is currently working in the system while building awareness of the next

---

[5]Ken Davey, University of Birmingham.

generation of issues to be tackled. Many of the best-performing projects build on contextual knowledge and a shared vision of the issues gained in earlier projects to move toward a more ambitious follow-on operation.

Whether or not decentralization is involved, there is always a political dimension in projects that benefit local governments. Although it is impossible to avoid changes of government, loss of project sponsors, or local government election cycles, project designs should seek to reduce vulnerability to these dynamics. Simplicity is one of the important safeguards. Ex-ante transparency on subsidies is another. For example, if funds are passed on with no discussion of how foreign exchange risk is to be handled, currency fluctuations can cause tensions with whoever bears the actual cost.

It is as important to be prepared for upside risks as it is to worry about the downside in project design. Some projects were less successful than they could have been, because they did not offer the flexibility to respond well to positive developments, such as an interest rate decline or the appearance of alternative funding sources. Such problems are manageable if they are taken into account in project design or if local partners are empowered to respond flexibly to new opportunities.

Future Issues

The recommendation to rebuild the UIF business line rests on a solid foundation of good project performance, as measured by the World Bank's independent evaluations. A number of models have emerged that have worked well in a variety of circumstances. The lessons learned from experience also indicate a substantive agenda to be addressed if the World Bank is not only to do more of these projects but also to do them better, by tailoring them to emerging needs.

Some of the key operational issues to be addressed follow:

- creating an appropriate distance between a central government and municipalities (sovereign guarantee and foreign exchange risk)
- responding to the diverse needs and capacities of the municipalities within a single country
- measuring results with more rigor (which should include assessing both the quality of subprojects and the evolution of municipal access to funding and their capital investment programs)
- treating subsidies for urban infrastructure more flexibly and explicitly in UIFs
- designing funds that are "user friendly" to municipal borrowers and that make it easy for financiers to "crowd in" with additional finance

Future Research and Analysis

In the course of the review, important knowledge gaps were identified. Research in the following areas is recommended:

- What is the experience of other donors with their UIF operations? What evidence is there of the impact of UIFs on overall infrastructure investment in small and medium cities? What are the other sources of funds available to them, and do UIFs leverage or substitute for these other sources?
- What have technical assistance components in UIF projects achieved— for municipalities, for intermediary institutions, and for the system of infrastructure finance? How well has technical assistance responded to the new demands arising from decentralization?
- What types of incentives for better local financial management have been built into UIF programs, and what is the track record of different instruments to enhance municipal performance (for example, performance grants, municipal contracts, and interest-rate subsidies)?
- How has intergovernmental reform affected the level and quality of investments in municipalities?
- How has financial sector reform affected the level and quality of investments in municipalities?

CHAPTER 1

Introduction and Objective

This book takes a look at the past to gain insights for the future. Nearly 30 years ago, in 1979, when the world urban population was only about half of the 3 billion that it is today, when most less developed countries (LDCs) were primarily rural, and before the wave of decentralization of the 1980s and 1990s, the World Bank started working with a new instrument with great potential.[1] The key characteristics of this instrument, the urban infrastructure fund (UIFs) are several.[2] It provides finance to improve a range of urban services, not just one sector, such as water and sanitation, leaving flexibility for local beneficiaries to set their priorities. They operate in more than one city. Perhaps the most important distinctive feature is that these projects use local institutions to do the work of identifying appraising and channeling finance to subnational entities (municipalities, local utilities, or community groups) on behalf of the World Bank.[3] This arrangement makes it feasible to reach beyond the

---

[1]These funds had been used by other donors such as the United States Agency for International Development (USAID) by this time. See Davey (1988).

[2]Urban infrastructure funds are also commonly referred to as municipal development funds (MDFs). However, some of the decentralized infrastructure finance projects not only targeted municipalities as beneficiaries, but also included local community groups or nongovernmental organizations (NGOs), for example, as sponsors of local infrastructure projects. For this reason, the less common, but more comprehensive terminology was used in this book.

[3]The scope of the empirical work in this book is limited to World Bank projects, and hence conclusions are drawn with reference to the World Bank. This limitation of scope in no sense implies a judgment as to the relevance of these conclusions or lack thereof for other international institutions. That subject is one subject that should be explored in further work. The World Bank and other international financial institutions could benefit from pooling their experiences in this area.

major capitals or business centers such as Chongqing, Mumbai, or São Paulo, or even regional capitals, to fund much smaller subprojects, which are suited to the capacities and needs of smaller cities and towns, because local agents are tasked with identifying and appraising these projects. This specialized function of reaching out to smaller cities and towns makes it practicable for a large donor such as the World Bank to reach small municipalities, but this function is typically necessary for any financier or government grant program. Reaching large numbers of municipalities with relatively small investment needs is a complex task that does not happen on its own. This capacity is fundamental to "scaling up" beyond small pilot projects to programs improving urban services with nationwide reach.

When use of UIFs began, reaching these clients was important for the governments concerned to give some balance—whether geographical, economic, or political—to their urban development efforts and to avoid unduly favoring their principal cities. Today these reasons continue to be valid and significant. However, the stakes are considerably higher now, because demographic trends place the bulk of expansion of urban population in smaller cities in developing countries. For the World Bank, expanding operational reach beyond major cities is central to its impact and relevance for the development agenda in the 21st century—the first urban century.

The Role of Demographics

A few stylized facts about future less developed country urbanization[4] illustrate this point.

- This year, 2008, the world will become 50 percent urban (see figure 1.1).
- Population growth over the next quarter-century will be primarily in cities, as the rural population is projected to stabilize (see figure 1.1).
- Nearly all urban growth will be in developing countries (see figure 1.2).
- Finally, and this is what is most interesting for the purposes of this analysis, the bulk of that growth in the nearer term,[5] amounting to roughly 750 million people—more than double the U.S. population—will not be in the highly visible megacities such as Dhaka and Lagos, but in smaller cities of fewer than 5 million people (see figure 1.3).

---

[4] United Nations (UN), World Urbanization Prospects Projections to 2030.

[5] City sizes are predicted through 2015; broader urban population aggregate projections are available through 2030.

Figure 1.1. Urban versus Rural Population Growth Worldwide through 2030

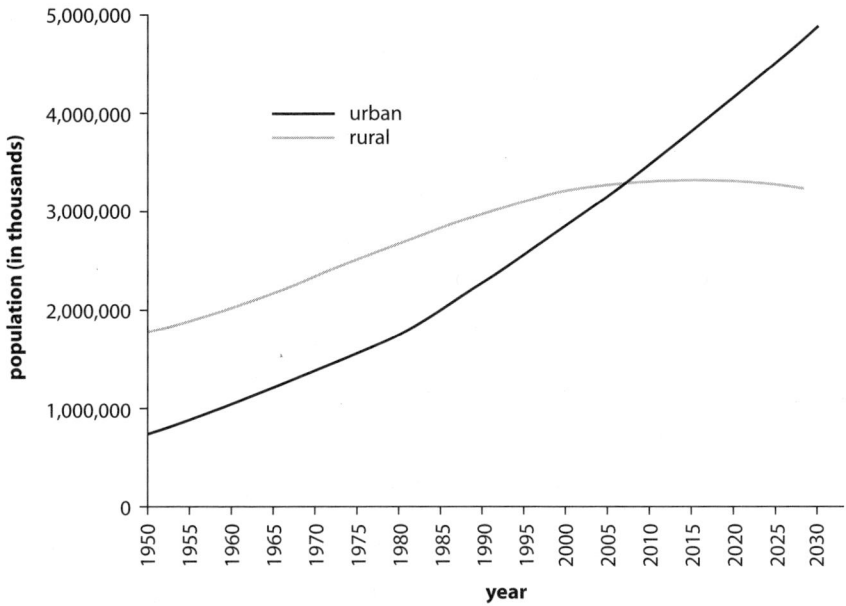

Source: United Nations: World Urbanization Prospects.

Figure 1.2. World Urban Population Growth through 2030: Low- and Middle-Income versus High-Income Countries

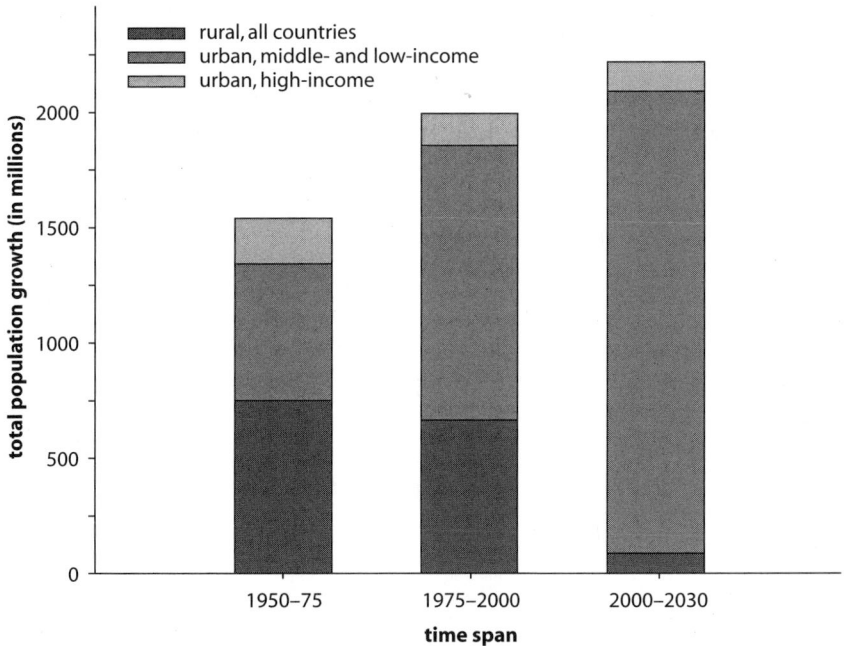

Source: United Nations: World Urbanization Prospects.

Figure 1.3. Distribution of World Urban Population Growth through 2015 by City Size

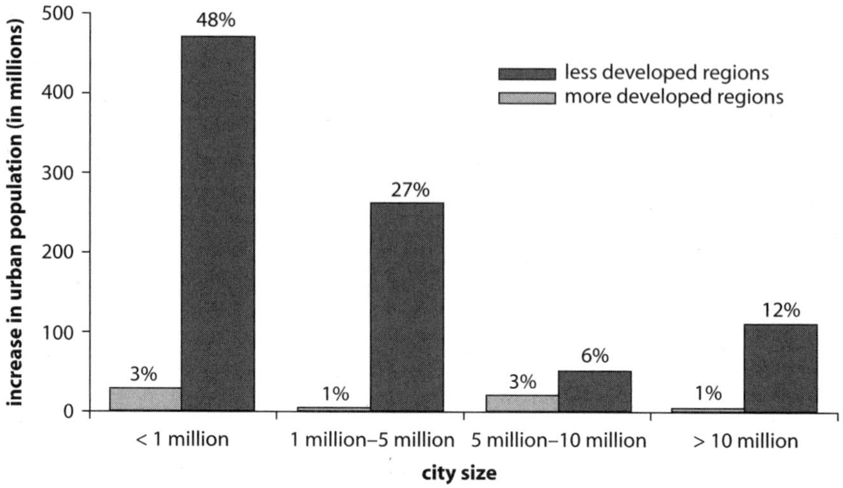

Source: United Nation, World Urbanization Prospects.

- This phenomenon is due in part to the common tendency for growth *rates* to decelerate in larger cities (see figure 1.4) as their absolute size grows.

These demographic trends imply massive investment needs in thousands of cities and towns that are relatively small now. As they grow, thousands of local governments will become an important part of the transition to modern economies. They will need to upgrade substantially to provide the types of infrastructure service that are essential for both productivity and quality of life in dense urban environments. **To get a sense of how dramatic a structural transformation this will be, note that in the United States the fixed capital stock of state and local governments was estimated to be twice that of the federal government: $1.9 trillion, or about 45 percent of gross domestic product (GDP) in 1985 (Boxkin et al. 1987).**

IFIs will need to adapt to be relevant in meeting these needs. Development projects should continue to service the very substantial populations already in mega-cities, and the World Bank's Development Policy Loans (DPLs) and standard investment loans are tailored to these clients' requirements. But to reach thousands of smaller urban centers, the World Bank must work with partners that can retail World Bank assis-

Figure 1.4. Selected Mega Cities' Growth Rates through 2010

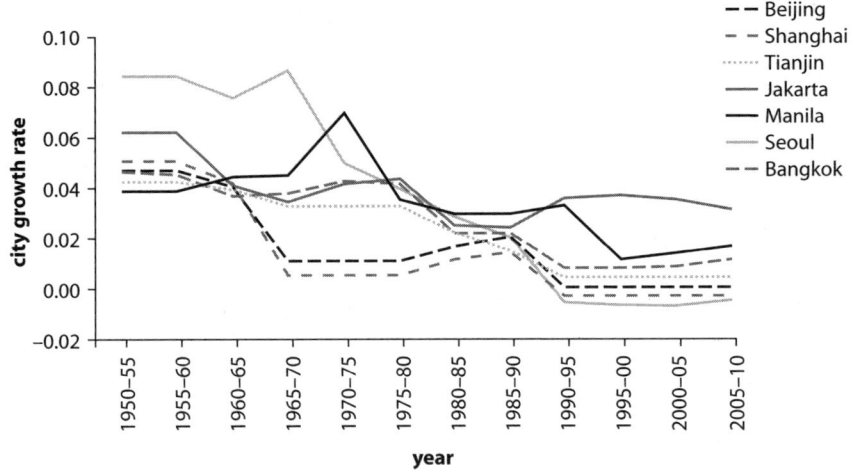

Source: United Nation, World Urbanization Prospects.

Note: Data until 2000 is based on estimates. Data after 2000 is based on projections.

tance to meet widely dispersed needs for investment and strengthening local institutions. Urban infrastructure funds, properly structured, have a greatly underused potential to play this important role.

The Role of Decentralization

Since the late 1980s, most countries have adopted some form of decentralization. This process has many dimensions and nuances specific to each country. Nonetheless, it often has the common feature of creating local governments with some responsibilities or expanding the roles of existing local governments, while also providing some sources of funding. Beyond that, the variety is enormous in that funding is often meager in relation to responsibilities; functional roles are often poorly defined or fragmented; administrative decisions may be tightly controlled; spending may be heavily earmarked; and so forth. More often than not, de facto decentralization is not as substantive as it seems de jure. Dramatic changes in the financial position of local governments following decentralization have been exceptional.

Yet as decentralization is formalized, local governments become players in the provision of local services, and the World Bank and other IFIs need to engage these governments as partners in meeting development objectives. Municipal development funds (MDFs), in particular, have been designed to provide such engagement. Even governments that have devolved very little responsibility or resources to local government have created institutions that finance and assist their local governments. Noteworthy examples are France (for roughly 160 years prior to decentralization) and Tunisia. Decentralization is an additional driver of demand for UIFs, especially as the process unrolls over the long run. But political and administrative decentralization is far from a necessary precondition for establishing institutions to reach out to the smaller cities and towns that will absorb the bulk of future urban population growth. Moreover, whereas decentralization may well increase the capital needs of local governments, it has not necessarily delivered the fiscal means for meeting those needs.

The Role of Financial Liberalization

Most countries have undertaken various forms of financial liberalization since the late 1980s. The wealthy Western European countries were among the first in this wave; they dismantled systems of captive savings and directed credit that had survived for decades during the prosperous period following the two World Wars. Developing countries, with weaker institutions and much lower incomes, followed rapidly as countries opened up to foreign investments, constraints on the banking sectors were lifted, capital markets were liberalized, and specialized directed credit institutions fell into disfavor—and many were restructured or wound down.

This liberalization offers opportunities to subnational governments in developing countries in the long run. Investors need assets with stable long-term returns, and lending for many municipal services can provide such assets. Thus, it makes sense to foster participation of local governments in financial markets. However, one of the lessons of financial sector reform is that the structural changes that bring demanders of capital together with suppliers around the world take much longer than a few years, especially when intermediated by as intensely political a process as decentralization. It will not be sufficient to liberalize the supply side and expect local governments to meet all their funding needs in financial markets. Government involvement will be a necessity, and well-structured funds can shape that involvement productively.

Objective of this Review of Experience

In view of the urgent need to develop instruments to reach out to urban local governments and finance decentralized infrastructure, this book seeks to understand the nearly 30 years of World Bank experience with UIFs. It traces the history and evolution of UIFs, examines performance indicators, and identifies the strengths and weaknesses of different models that have emerged. Based upon a detailed review of a recent set of completed projects, the book discusses specific lessons drawn from this experience.

For the purposes of the statistical analysis in this study, we identified and analyzed World Bank UIF projects from the early 1970s to fiscal year (FY) 2006. Appendix 1 describes in detail how these projects were identified and the database that was created. This subset of World Bank projects includes 104 operations managed by the Urban Development (UD) and other sector boards.[6] The total commitment amount in 2006 constant dollar terms covered by the sample is $10.9 billion.[7] A breakdown by region is shown in table 1.1.

Table 1.1. UIFs by Region

		UIF Projects	
Region	Number of Projects	(US $ million (Constant 2006))	% of Total WB Projects by Value
AFR	22	1,140	1.0
EAP	11	1,945	1.1
ECA	12	547	0.5
LCR	34	4, 340	2.2
MNA	11	828	1.6
SAR	14	2,071	1.5
Total	**104**	**10,872**	**1.4**

Source: Authors' calculations. See appendix 1 for further details.

---

[6]As appendix 1 explains in more detail, to identify UIFs, the authors searched for any projects with urban and municipal themes. As a result, projects managed by a number of sector boards, such as rural development, were included in the group. If a rural development project was financing municipal infrastructure and was treating the urban theme, it was included. Appendix 2 lists all projects identified as UIFs.

[7]Because the time series examined covers nearly 30 years, large distortions would be introduced by examining a time series without correction for inflation. Accordingly, the nominal U.S. dollar amounts were deflated using the U.S. gross domestic product (GDP) deflator.

Although the dollar commitments represent significant sums, this line of business accounts for only a small share of World Bank lending in all regions. This suggests that it should be possible to expand this line of business substantially with little disruption of other lines of business. The small percentages dedicated to local infrastructure retailed outside of major cities also suggest that substantially more effort may be warranted.

CHAPTER 2

Trends and Structure of Urban Infrastructure Funds

The first projects in which the World Bank worked directly with municipal governments were line of credit operations. They were based largely on the development finance company model used earlier for directed credits to industrial borrowers, small and medium enterprises, and farmers, among others. As shown in figure 2.1, the majority of these UIF projects (about 60 percent by US$ volume) are classified as Urban Development (UD) sector board, although the Social Protection (SP) and Rural Development (RDV) sector boards have also played a role. The other sector boards include Financial Sector (FS), Water Supply and Sanitation (WSS), Social Development (SDV), and Private Sector Development (PSD), but these represent only a handful of projects. Thirty-three percent of the projects by value were in the Latin America and the Caribbean Region (LAC). Except for LAC, the UD sector board dominates lending by volume in other regions. Because the RDV and SP projects tend to be much smaller, there is less UD dominance in the number of projects.

Figure 2.2 illustrates the wide geographic scope of the urban infrastructure funds by country. They have been used in a number of countries, covering both large and small borrowers. Although the dollar commitment volume is relatively small in Africa, this reflects much more the small project size in Africa, rather than the number of projects, as shown in table 1.1.

Figure 2.1. UIF Commitments by Region and Sector Board

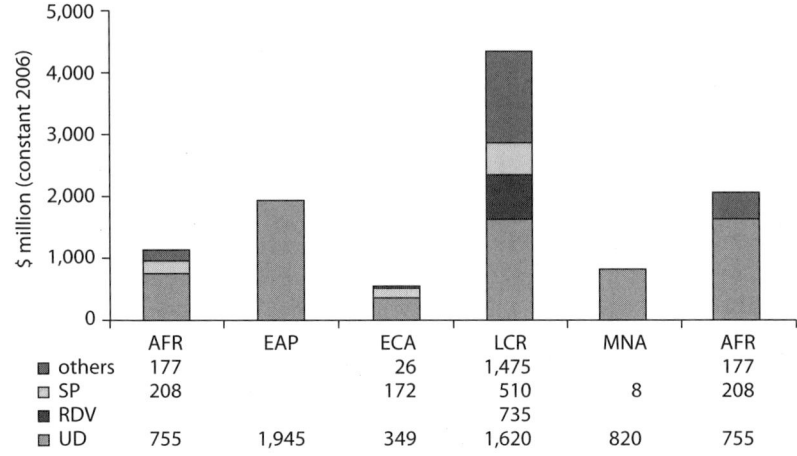

	AFR	EAP	ECA	LCR	MNA	AFR
■ others	177		26	1,475		177
□ SP	208		172	510	8	208
■ RDV				735		
□ UD	755	1,945	349	1,620	820	755

Source: Authors' calculations. See appendix 1 for further details.
*Others includes Environment, Financial Sector, Public Sector, Governance, Private Sector Development, Social Development, Transport, Water Supply and Sanitation Sector Boards.

Figure 2.2. UIF Commitments by Country, $ (Constant 2006) Million

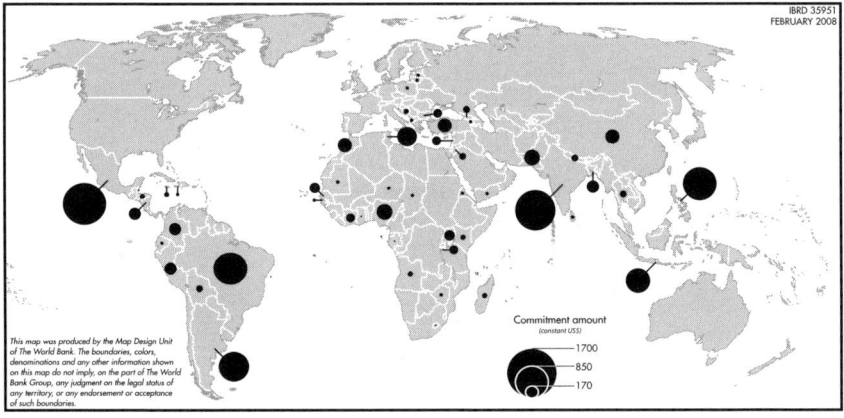

Source: Authors' calculations. See appendix 1 for further details.

Composition of UIFs by Sector Board over Time

Urban Development was virtually the only sector board that managed UIF projects until 1991, after which SD and RDV became more significant. Quite recently, UD has again come to be the dominant sector board for these projects. This trend can be seen in figure 2.3. It is interesting to note, too, that community participation in project selection was pioneered by the UD sector board for Indonesia in 1981, two years after

Figure 2.3. Annual UIF Commitments by Sector Board

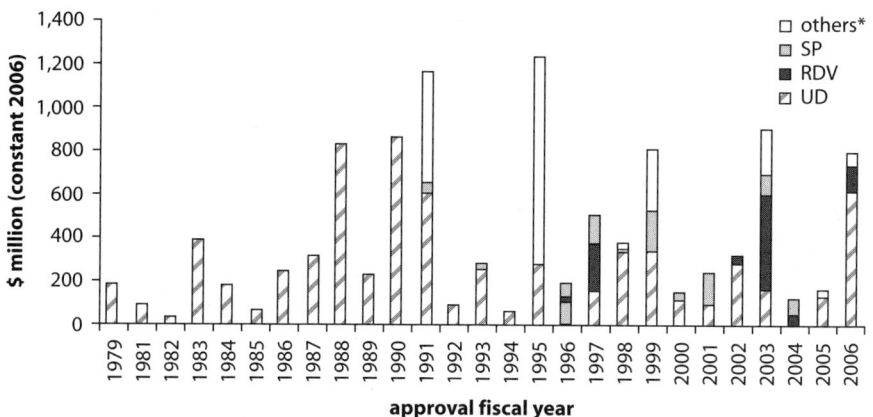

Source: Authors' calculations. See Appendix 1 for further details.
*Others includes Environment, Financial Sector, Public Sector, Governance, Private Sector Development, Social Development, Transport, Water Supply and Sanitation Boards.

the UIF instrument was introduced. Likewise, the first project promoting access to private finance for local governments was an urban project approved in 1988 for Nigeria.

Long-Term Trends in the Volume of UIF Lending

As shown in figure 2.3, annual UIF lending fluctuates considerably. It is easier to understand longer-term trends from five-year annual averages, as shown in figure 2.4. Lending volume of UIFs stopped growing and

Figure 2.4. Trends in Total Urban Infrastructure Fund Lending—Annual Averages

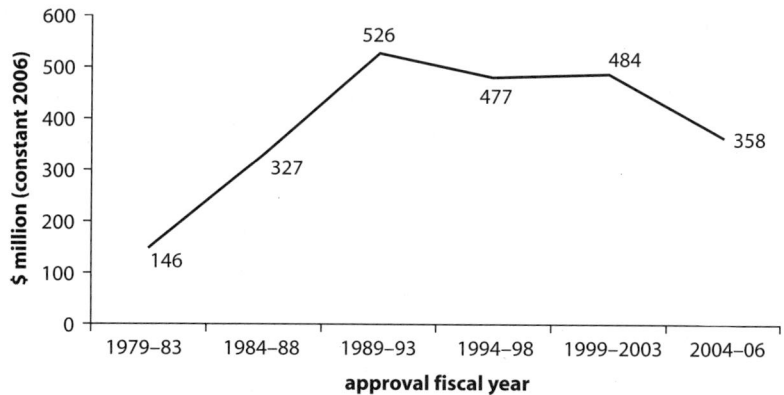

Source: Authors' Calculations. See Appendix 1 for further details.

even declined since the early 1990s, after rapid increases in the first few years of lending. **This trend is noteworthy because, just as decentralization became a global phenomenon and as urban populations are rising rapidly, operations in a critical, related area are stagnating.**

This is the case in spite of the arrival of social funds in the 1990s and in spite of the more recent Infrastructure Action Plan (IAP), meant to reinvigorate infrastructure lending. Figure 2.5 shows a breakdown of UIFs between Infrastructure Sectors and others, mostly social funds. The rise of the latter type of operation blunted but never fully compensated for the rapid decline of Urban Development lending for UIFs, which forms the mainstay of UIFs in the infrastructure sector. By the same token, the dramatic drop of the social funds in the last few years, to less than a third of their peak value, has not been fully compensated by a reprise of UIF projects from the infrastructure sectors, which have only increased by about 40 percent since the establishment of the IAP. For example, UIF approvals by the UD sector board since the beginning of the Infrastructure Action Plan are averaging about US$270 million per annum, somewhat more than half of the annual average for the 1989–93 period.

Figure 2.6 shows that lending values are stagnating in part because the average project size declined dramatically in the mid-1990s. The recent

Figure 2.5. Trends in Annual Average Urban Infrastructure Fund Lending by Infrastructure and Non-infrastructure Sector Boards

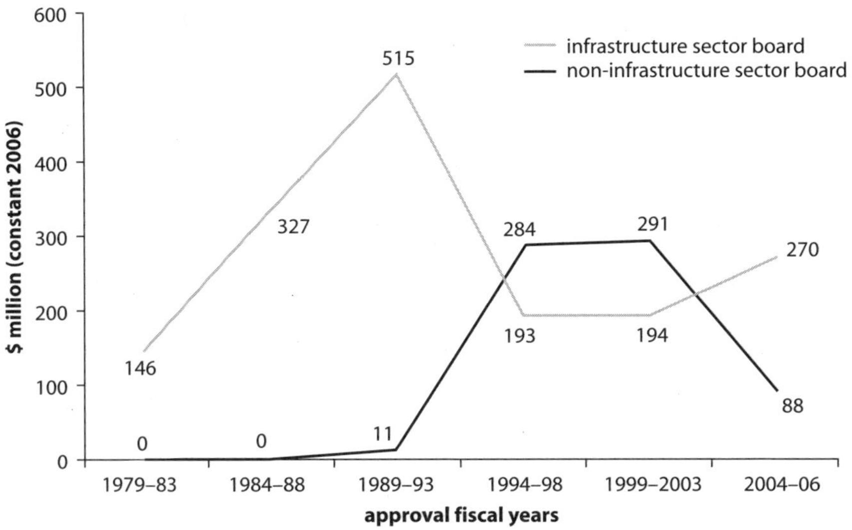

Source: Authors' calculations. See appendix 1 for further details.

Figure 2.6. Trends in Annual Average Project Size

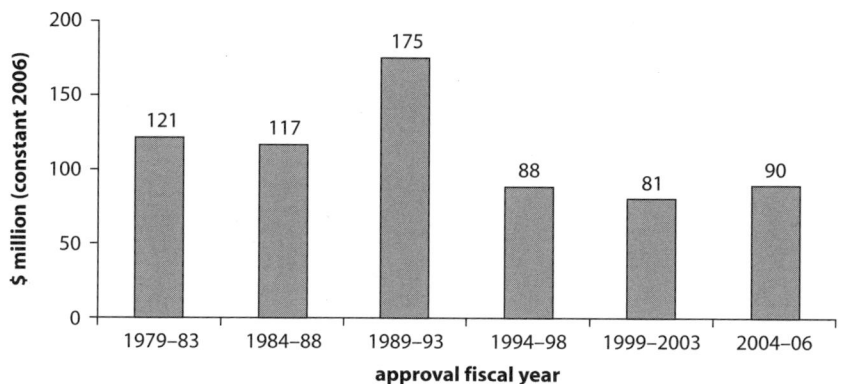

Source: Authors' calculations. See appendix 1 for further details.

partial rebound in project size is not sufficient to bring real lending values near their peak.

Although the overall decline in project size may explain some of the decline in UIFs, an additional explanation may be the decline in lending to middle-income countries (MICs). The secular decline in UIFs was primarily on the side of the International Bank for Reconstruction and Development (IBRD), although the World Bank's International Development Association (IDA) lending for urban funds has shown weakness in recent years as well. IBRD UIFs have declined more steeply than IDA projects. All IBRD lending by the UD sector board has also declined, but not as dramatically as UIF funds. The UIF tool has suffered in relation to overall Urban Development lending.[1]

This stagnation is partly attributable to the move away from line of credit operations more generally across the World Bank. Such projects on-lend World Bank funds or offer a blend of grants and loans for specific development objectives. As early as 1989, the "Levy report"[2] spelled out concerns that credit directed to specific sectors or borrowers through intermediaries sponsored by governments impeded the development of the broader financial sector. Later Operational Directive (OD) 8.30[3]

---

[1] These figures exclude financing for local intermediaries supporting local governments provided by other parts of the World Bank Group, notably the International Finance Corporation (IFC) and the Multilateral Investment Guarantee Agency (MIGA). Thus far, however, the amounts they have provided are modest.

[2] *Report on the Task Force on Financial Sector Operations* R98-163. World Bank, August 1, 1989.

[3] Now succeeded by Operational Policy (OP) and Bank Policy (BP) 8.30.

Figure 2.7. UIF Lending Projects

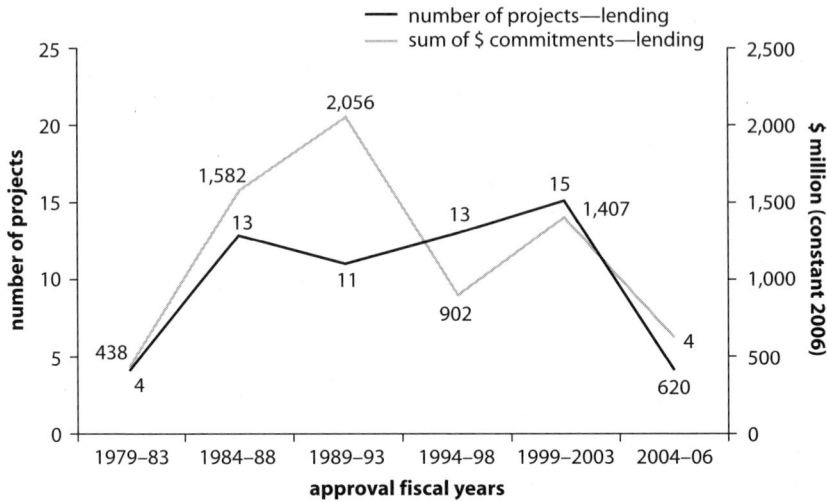

Source: Authors' calculations. See appendix 1 for further details.

Figure 2.8. UIF Grant Projects

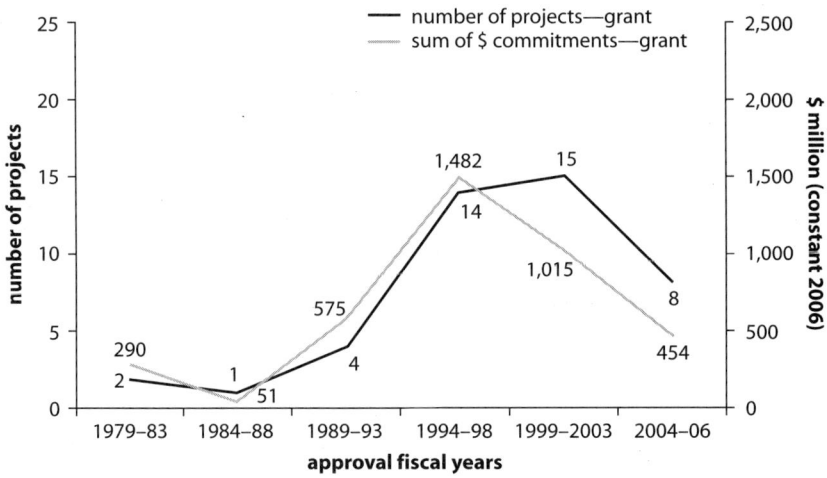

Source: Authors' calculations. See appendix 1 for further details.

placed strict conditions for undertaking line of credit operations. The grant projects are not seen to have the same negative impact on the financial sector, and they also tend to be smaller than the loan products. These grant-based products have played a more significant role over the years. Figures 2.7 and 2.8, which track the evolution of grant-based and lending based UIFs, show that grants surged just as the products that on-lent fell. But total lending for UIFs has also declined.

Other IFIs apparently did not turn away from directed credit with the same vigor as the World Bank. The Operations Evaluation Department (2005a) found that, from 1993 through 2003, the World Bank lost market share in the line of credit (LOC) business generally. Yet, as discussed in the next chapter, the UIF product has performed well among LOCs. UIFs have not suffered nearly as much from the problems that plagued other World Bank lines of credit, but they have fallen out of favor along with them. The reduction in credit operations for local governments that followed the shift from directed credit more generally was built on implicit assumptions that turned out to be overoptimistic. Financial sector liberalization and decentralization have proven far from sufficient to ensure local governments' access to adequate capital finance. The trend of decline of the UIF instrument with high potential should be reversed. The World Bank cannot afford to miss opportunities to reach out to local governments that have now become critical to the World Bank's impact and relevance. With more than 30 years of experience in UIFs that have experimented with a variety of different models, the World Bank is positioned now to reinvigorate this type of lending, with products better tailored to the variety of opportunities and constraints facing its clients.

CHAPTER 3

Performance of UIFs

Whether offering loans or grants, urban infrastructure funds (UIFs) have performed well in World Bank evaluations and compare favorably with other lines of credit in important respects. Figure 3.1 summarizes the performance of UIFs in outcome ratings in comparison with all World Bank projects, as well as a sample of lines of credit examined by the Operations Evaulation Department (OED) (2005b). **This shows that UIFs perform somewhat above the average for the entire World Bank portfolio. More importantly, they perform substantially better than the sample of projects offering lines of credit studied by OED.**

Figure 3.2 breaks out performance of UIFs by sector board, and then compares the results with all projects managed by that same sector board as assessed by the Independent Evaluation Group (IEG) (previously OED). The figure shows the percentage of projects that were rated either "highly satisfactory" or "satisfactory." This is a higher standard than total "satisfactory" projects, because the "marginally satisfactory" category is excluded.

The performance of the UIFs of the Urban Development (UD) sector board is very close to overall UD project performance and above average for the World Bank. The same is true of the Social Protection (SP) sector board's UIF projects. The Rural Development (RDV) UIF funds strongly outperform their sector overall, and the "other" group of UIFs underperforms the overall sector board results, but with 10 projects each, both samples are very small. It is interesting that the UD funds projects have "fat tails" (that is, a relatively large percentage of projects with both strong and poor performance). UD has a higher percentage of poorly

Figure 3.1. Outcome Ratings for UIFs

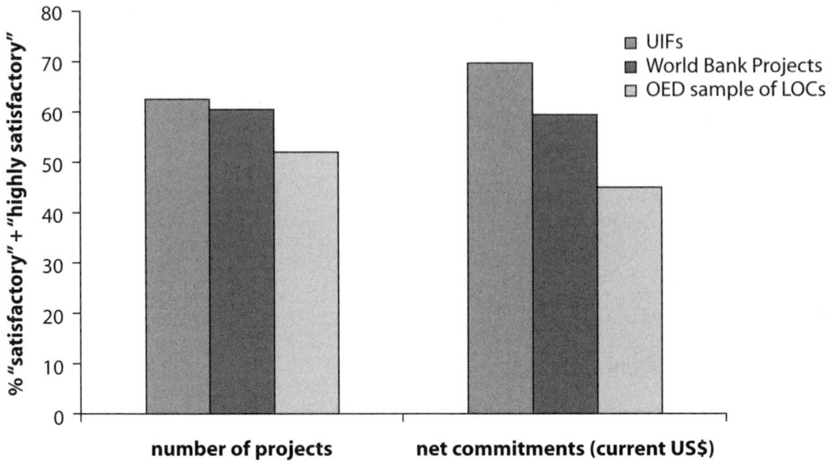

Source: Authors' calculations. See appendix 1 for further details. OED (2005b) and World Bank internal data.

Figure 3.2. Selected Outcome Ratings for UIFs by Sector Board

HS+S	HU+U		
61%	25%	**UD**	**UIFs**
100%	**0%**	RDV	
54%	15%	**SP**	
50%	**17%**	others	
63%	22%	**UD**	**All World Bank Projects**
55%	**32%**	RDV	
59%	15%	**SP**	
62%	**23%**	others	

Source: Authors' calculations. See appendix 1 for further details. IEG Database of Project Evaluations.

Note: HS "highly satisfactory," HU "highly unsatisfactory," S "satisfactory," and U "unsatisfactory."

performing UIFs because they handle nearly all of the lending projects. (Only one of the "unsatisfactory" group of UIF projects provided grants rather than loans.) **As the discussion below will show, lessons from both good and bad projects indicate that the downside risks that UIFs have encountered are both identifiable and manageable.**

The OED study of lines of credit identified certain problem areas for these projects: poor disbursement records and poor tracking of repay-

Figure 3.3. Disbursements as a Percentage of Commitments for UIFs

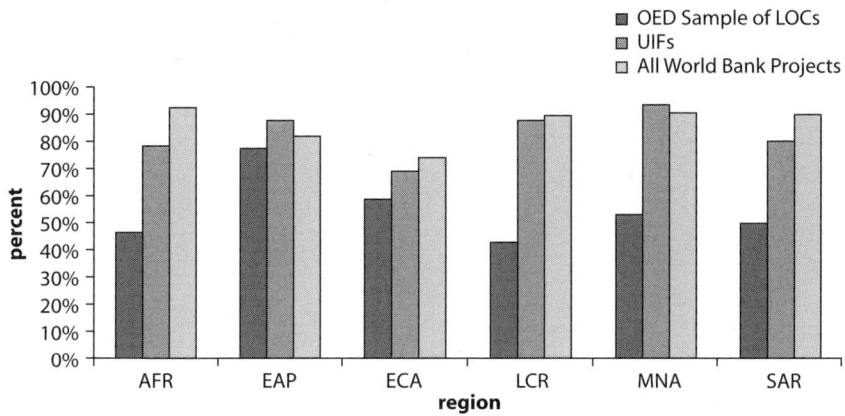

Source: Authors' Calculations. See Appendix 1 for further details. OED (2005b) and World Bank internal data.

ment rates. The track record of UIFs in these areas is examined below. **As can be seen from figure 3.3, the UIFs have a much stronger performance in terms of disbursements than the line of credit sample studied by OED. In some regions, the UIF disbursements are comparable to or better than the overall World Bank portfolio.**

With respect to reporting on repayments, UIFs do not fare as well (figure 3.4). For those UIFs extending credit, performance in tracking and reporting on loan recoveries is a bit worse than the entire line of credit sample, in which only half of the projects reported loan repayment rates. It should be noted that, among those UIFs reporting recoveries, 67 percent had recoveries greater than 90 percent. In comparison with other directed lines of credit, this performance is very good. Independent institutions·serving as intermediaries had a wider spread of recovery outcomes than government institutions, but no clear-cut overall superiority.

In summary, UIFs have performed well. The percentage of UIFs that is "highly satisfactory" or "fully satisfactory" is above the average for all World Bank projects.[1] Compared with other intermediary projects, UIFs have performed considerably better. **This experience indicates that UIFs**

---

[1] The term *"satisfactory" projects,* as defined here, explicitly excludes those projects rated "marginally satisfactory" by IEG. The analysis sought to consider performance as a potential reason for the decline in UIF projects, and therefore looked at the percentage of "fully satisfactory" and "highly satisfactory" projects. It would be understandable that UIF operations in this area might be reduced if "satisfactory" projects tended to be only "marginally satisfactory." This is not the case.

Figure 3.4. Loan Recoveries in UIFs: Reporting and Repayment Rates by Institutional Arrangement

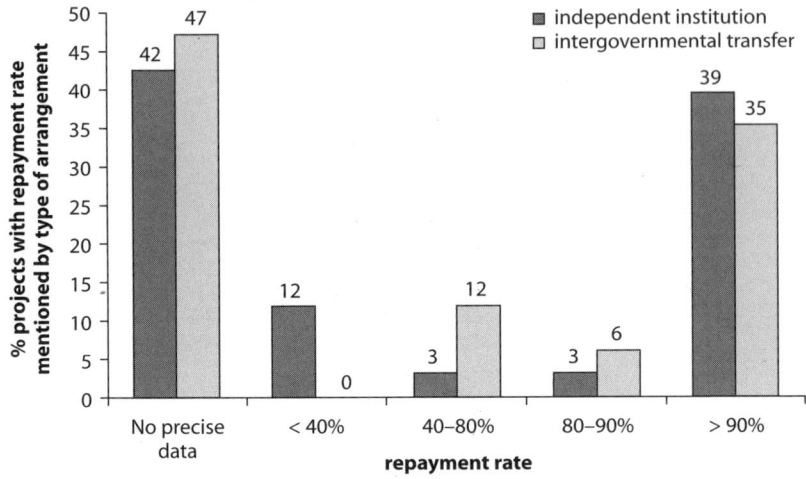

Source: Authors' calculations. See appendix 1 for further details. OED (2005b) and World Bank internal data.

hold promise for responding to new demographic patterns and emerging infrastructure demands and should thus be pursued more proactively to reverse the stagnation and decline of the past 15 years. The following chapters move beyond summary outcome ratings to explore UIF models in more detail, to understand better the elements that make for successful projects.

CHAPTER 4

UIF Design:
Options for Intermediation Strategy

Every World Bank project that seeks to support municipal infrastructure investment in multiple cities requires an intermediating structure of some kind, simply to make the project administratively manageable. The institution that performs the intermediation function can leave a lasting imprint on a country's municipal infrastructure sector. The rules it follows set a precedent for future domestic financing, and the institution itself may be designed to become a sustainable feature of municipal finance and local investment. For this reason, the intermediation structure is crucial to program design, and the appropriate design choices should reflect, among others, the state of both the financial system and the capacities of local governments.

There are many design alternatives for intermediation of multisite urban infrastructure investment programs. Four categories of design choice merit particular attention here:

- *The type and scale of investment works that will be built.* "Local" investment projects may range in scale from neighborhood footpaths or public latrines, on the one hand, to major road construction or metropolitan-scale water supply systems, on the other, with a vast range of alternatives in between.
- *The process of priority-setting for subprojects.* Priorities for local investment may be set at the central level by central ministries or other agencies, at the municipal level through capital planning or other

means, at the community level through participatory processes leading to community-driven demand, or through combinations of these alternatives.

- *The financing mechanism connecting central authorities with the local investment subprojects.* Funds from World Bank projects may reach end users through specific-purpose grants, block grants, loans (market rate or subsidized), or a mix of these instruments.
- *The administrative and political character of intermediary and oversight institutions.* Programs may be administered by agencies that are part of central government administration, by independent organizations of various types, or by for-profit financial institutions. The administering structure may be organized as a single central organization or as a decentralized collection of local institutions.

Two Models of Intermediation

The World Bank's approach to urban infrastructure funds (UIFs) has spanned a continuum between two polar models of intermediation: credit institutions that on-lend and small grant/social funds. In this sense, the group of UIFs is quite distinct from traditional lines of credit that follow the credit and on-lending model uniquely. The coexistence of these two models among UIFs is a necessity given the nature of the clients for decentralized infrastructure finance. Many local governments are prohibited by law from borrowing. In some other cases, central governments are unwilling to offer funding for urban infrastructure on anything but a lending basis, nominally on market terms. In yet others, the World Bank or the government wishes to use the design of the UIF as a means of targeting spending for local infrastructure to poor beneficiaries, but wants to improve the efficiency of the grant system.

Projects often identify their goals as moving from the status quo to a closer approximation of one or the other of these models. The choice of models has significant implications for program priorities, and it is worthwhile spelling out the principal differences.

Model I: Market-Driven Credit Institutions and On-Lending

In mature market economies, the task of delegated monitoring of local government infrastructure investments typically is assigned to financial institutions. A lending institution is expected to raise financing on the capital market at market rates, provide credit for investments at market rates of interest adjusted for credit risk, and then monitor both project execution and credit risk. This model of intermediation applies to commercial banks and to specialized institutions such as municipal development banks that lend to local governments for infrastructure investments.

A variant of the model, found in the United States and other countries that finance municipal investments primarily through local bond markets, separates the task of monitoring credit and project risk from the task of supplying capital. Credit rating agencies and bond guarantee institutions perform the intermediation task of assessing risk and monitoring project performance on behalf of the investors who supply capital. When the market model of financial intermediation succeeds, it provides a sustainable channel connecting the special infrastructure investment needs of municipalities with broader financial markets, thus allowing local governments to tap private savings to smooth the fiscal demands of lumpy investment projects.

A reform program that seeks to move toward this model typically attempts to strengthen the market orientation of existing financial institutions that lend for municipal infrastructure investment or establishes a new on-lending institution that is intended to evolve into a market-oriented intermediary. The process may involve liberalization of traditional government finance institutions, coupled with the introduction of private-market competition. Or it may involve extending the market reach of private commercial banks to include provision of longer-term credits to municipal governments. Box 4.1 illustrates how the transition from a monopolistic and subsidized directed credit agency to private municipal market access was made in France, starting in the early 19th century.

Underpinning the successful implementation of this model is an intergovernmental finance and governance structure that gives local governments the financial capacity and administrative autonomy to participate in financial markets meaningfully. Decentralization is widespread, but not universal, and it is increasingly recognized to be a long-term process rather than a single discrete reform. Thus, many of the World Bank's borrowers find themselves in different states of readiness for making the transition to the full-market model. Accordingly, UIFs working with local governments typically have sought to advance an intergovernmental finance and municipal reform agenda as part of the project objectives, while recognizing that the limitations imposed by the existing institutional arrangements could not be eliminated overnight.

Box 4.1

A Model of Market-Oriented Reform: Crédit Local de France

The transformation of Crédit Local de France (CLF, now Dexia) exemplifies the process of market reform of a government finance institution. It provides the implicit model for reform designs supported by the World Bank in several French-speaking African nations as well as elsewhere.

Historically, Crédit Local de France was a monopolistic supplier of capital to the French municipal sector. The predecessor of CLF drew its financing from preferential access to savings accumulated in the small-saver postal system. It enjoyed a below-market cost of capital and lent to municipalities at below-market rates of interest. As a municipal bank, CLF also helped municipalities with project preparation, feasibility studies, capital budgeting, and general financial management. CLF was a public bank, owned by the French government.

Starting in the 1980s, CLF was restructured to fit into a competitive market. The first step in this process involved clarification that CLF loans to municipalities were not protected by implicit government guarantees, as had been common practice. This forced CLF to undertake more prudent credit-risk assessments. Next, CLF lost its preferential access to small-saver savings as part of a more general dismantling of directed credit in the financial system. CLF was forced to raise financing through bond issues and became one of the largest bond issuers in the world. Finally, starting in 1993, ownership of CLF was privatized by selling government shares in the market. The sale took place in tranches until CLF was 100 percent privatized.

As anticipated, the loss of CLF's monopoly position introduced competition into the municipal lending sector. By 1995, for example, CLF accounted for 42 percent of local authority lending in the French market, where it faced competition both from commercial banks and an emerging municipal bond market. CLF has thrived in the competitive environment, acquiring other municipal banks throughout Western and Central Europe and becoming a pan-European institution that provides both financing and, where desired by municipalities, assistance in project preparation and capital budgeting, under separate compensation agreements. It also has diversified its banking services beyond the municipal sector.

Promoting a transition to the competitive private-municipal-credit model is among the implicit objectives of World Bank Operational Policy (OP) 8.30 and the preceding financial sector work, notably the Levy report. Following the Levy report and OP and (World) Bank Policy (BP) 8.30, there was a strong shift toward supporting fundamental financial sector reform and promoting private sector finance (rather than working largely within the limitations of the existing system) as necessary objectives of any line of credit. This change added to the sectoral reform agenda facing UIF operations and pushed them to address structural issues in the financial sector. This constituted a substantial movement beyond the important agenda of intergovernmental relations and municipal finance and governance that were already necessarily a part of UIFs whose beneficiaries were local governments. In sum, UIF operations often needed to address intergovernmental issues to build borrowing capacity, while OP and BP 8.30 also drove them to seek measures to support reform of the financial sector. The lending trends discussed earlier suggest that demanding these two ambitious objectives in a single operation has impeded the use of UIFs.

Model II: Poverty-Oriented Grant Financing of Community Works

At the other extreme of market-oriented credit institutions lending to creditworthy municipal governments are the poverty-oriented community works projects. These may be called *social funds*, especially when managed by the Social Protection network, but have also been managed by Rural Development as poverty-alleviation programs. As described on the World Bank web site for Social Protection,[1] these programs provide financing for "small-scale public investments targeted at meeting the needs of the poor and vulnerable communities." These funds are typically organized around the principle of community participation in project selection, project design, and operation and maintenance of works once they are built. The primary emphasis in early operations was getting assistance to the poor, who were affected by adjustment or economic shocks not expected to be permanent. Hence project design focused on creating capacity to achieve results on the ground quickly and credibly. Beyond the direct investment objectives, these projects, by using community participation in project selection, sought to build social capital rather than promote any sort of sector reform. Some early projects—the Peru Social Fund, for example—openly bypassed existing institutions,

---

[1]http://web.worldbank.org/WBSITE/EXTERNAL/TOPICS/EXTSOCIALPROTECTION/EXTSF/

local governments, and others. Follow-on projects, though, sought to redress this imbalance, as will be discussed below. Others, such as the Agence d'Exécution de Travaux d'Intérêt Public (AGETIP) projects in Africa, targeted local governments as the immediate beneficiaries, but nonetheless focused on achieving results on the ground quickly rather than institutional change and investment planning. In this sense, while many grant funds were also financing decentralized urban infrastructure, the product has often been radically different from most lines of credit, in terms of not only its approach, but also its ultimate objective.

The poor and vulnerable communities that are intended beneficiaries do not have the capacity to repay loans; as a result, almost all financing has been via grants in the social-fund model. Instead of banks or windows of government financial institutions as intermediating institutions, these funds work primarily through nongovernmental organizations (NGOs). They have sought to complement the provision of small community works with income-generating programs of various kinds, ranging from labor-intensive works that can employ community labor during construction to micro-enterprise lending and development of small- and medium-size enterprises that can specialize in the construction of small-scale public works. **However structured, there is one basic principle behind the grant fund model: making efficient use of government subsidies for capital investments that cannot be funded on fully commercial terms.**

The implementation principles embraced by this model have been widely incorporated into World Bank projects. An OED assessment found that by 2000, the proportion of all World Bank projects, including community participation elements, had risen to 67 percent.[2] Between 1973 and 1988, NGOs participated in only 5 percent of World Bank projects. By 2000, 71 percent of projects under preparation and appraisal had made provision for civil society involvement through some type of NGO.[3]

Table 4.1 provides a summary contrast of what we have termed the Financial Intermediation and Poverty-Oriented Grant Fund approaches to supporting municipal infrastructure projects in multiple urban sites. It is important to emphasize, however, that these represent the extremes of a continuum and are not normative models.

Activities supported by the Urban Development sector board have also adopted local participation from early days and have provided some grants. However, from the very start, Urban Development UIF projects

---

[2]World Bank, *Civil Society Relationships: Fiscal 2000 Progress Report* (2001).

[3]OED, *Participation Process Review* (World Bank: 2001).

Table 4.1. Financial Intermediation versus Poverty-Oriented Grants

Feature	Financial intermediation	Poverty-Oriented Grant Fund
Financial end user	Municipal government	Community NGO
Primary purposes	Strengthen municipal finance and municipal management, build infrastructure systems, and build sustainable credit market	Develop institutions to express community-driven demand, improve access of poor to basic services, and build community works
Financial instrument	Loans or mix of loans and grants	Grants
Typical scale of subprojects	> US$250,000	< US$10,000
Intermediating institutions	Commercial banks, Municipal Development Fund, Window of Ministry of Finance + Project Management Unit (PMU)	Apex NGO or AGETIP/Decentralized NGO Network

Source: Author compilation.

emphasized the financial intermediation model, in part because the World Bank has been reluctant to provide explicit subsidies for "urban" projects, while UIF projects implemented by Social Protection (SP) and Rural Development (RD) have adopted the grant model[4] (see figure 4.1). Although only a minority of UD projects have the express objective

Figure 4.1. Loan Financing versus Grant Financing of Subprojects by Sector Board

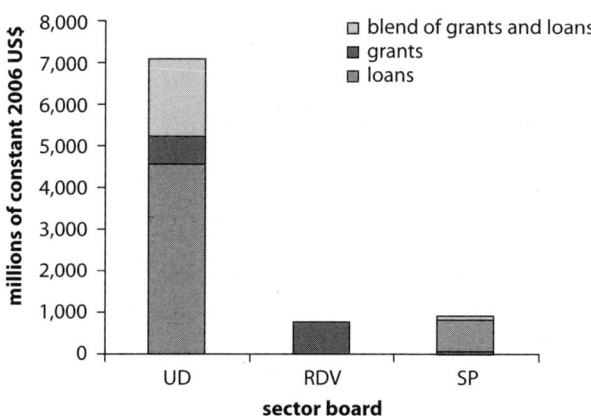

Source: Authors' calculations. See appendix 1 for further details.

---

[4]In practice, it is often quite difficult to distinguish the beneficiaries of, for example, an RD or SP UIF from those of a UD UIF.

of developing a sustainable, private sector credit market for local infrastructure finance (figures 4.2 and 4.3), many more Urban Development
projects set making the first steps toward establishing sustainable credit
financing as one of their immediate goals.

When, in the early 1990s, the World Bank started to shift emphasis to
improving the financial sector performance and move away from provid-

**Figure 4.2. Development Objective: Development of Municipal Credit Market
by Sector Board**

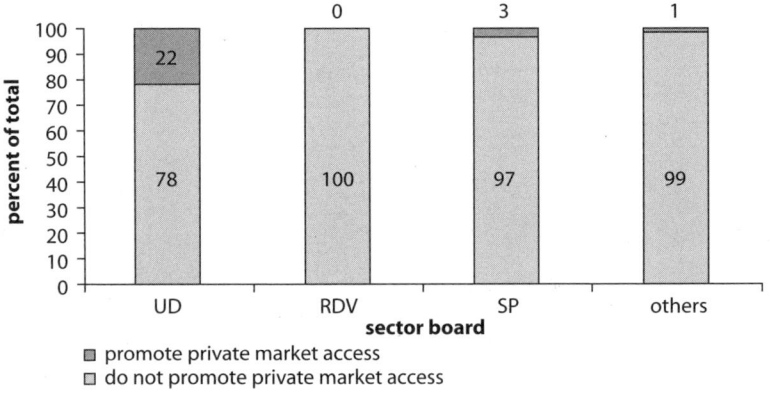

Source: Authors' calculations. See appendix 1 for further details.

Figure 4.3. Development Objective: Development of Municipal Credit Market over Time

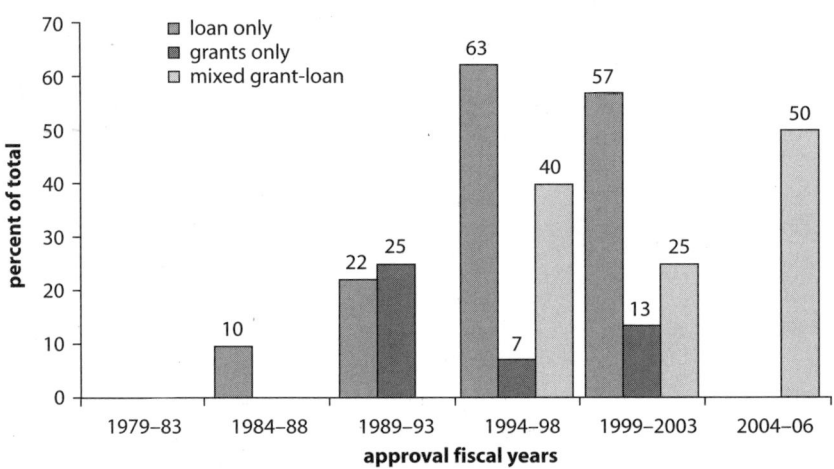

Source: Authors' calculations. See appendix 1 for further details.

ing credit to specific clients, Urban Development UIFs were caught in the crosswinds. Increasingly, such projects had to be justified with arguments about improving access to credit markets. Designing a project that ensured a rapid transition to private access became a necessary condition for supporting a municipal development fund (MDF). Figure 4.3 shows that the objective of establishing a sustainable private sector credit market for municipal infrastructure finance has increased in importance in recent years for Urban Development projects, accelerating in the early 1990s following the Levy report. Sometimes this approach worked, and sometimes it distorted project design, and the discussion of lessons of experience below provides examples. Experience with decentralization has now amply shown that this transition takes a long time, even in the best of circumstances. Box 4.1 provides an illustrative example from a high-income country.

The middle ground along the continuum between the social fund–type model and the market finance model became more difficult to occupy, as the rise of the poverty-oriented grant style UIFs illustrates. As a result, the World Bank presence in this area declined overall—and the choices available to World Bank clients—narrowed. As intermediation-style projects declined, far more direct grants were provided, some of which were seen as circumventing local government. The social funds did not replace the level of finance and engagement with local government provided by earlier generations of Urban Development projects, as was to be expected given their objectives. Yet operationally they were seen as substitutes and crowded out the older project model. Opportunities to offer UIF projects providing finance combined with institutional development for local governments when private-market access was not imminent dried up, even though this model was more adapted to the status of decentralization for a large number of World Bank clients. This polarity is less striking today, following the Infrastructure Action Plan, but, as figure 2.5 shows, the ground lost in the 1990s has not been recovered.

Revitalizing the UIF line of business with products tailored to specific client needs should be the priority now. Project design should be situated wherever is most suitable for the client along the continuum between the poverty alleviation grant model and the market-oriented financial intermediation model. The two models, rather than being seen as substitutes and competitors, should be viewed as complementary in country programs that demonstrate much stronger engagement to meet the array of needs arising in smaller cities and towns, as well as the vast differences in capacity between large secondary cities and small towns.

CHAPTER 5

Learning from Experience in Project Design

Over the past quarter-century, the World Bank has acquired a good deal of field experience with different project designs. This experience is most usefully reviewed by examining classes of countries facing similar economic conditions and similar choices in project design.

Transplanting the Line of Credit Model in Sub-Saharan Africa

The standard financial model was the first intermediation approach to be tried in Sub-Saharan Africa municipal infrastructure programs. These projects followed the successful "all-lending" urban infrastructure fund (UIF) projects in Latin America in the late 1970s and early 1980s, in which lines of credit disbursed quickly and repayment rates were excellent.[1]

Transplanting this model in Africa encountered problems. The difficulties experienced by the five projects in table 5.1 illustrate some of the typical risks in the lending model. The goals, as expressed explicitly in several of the programs, were to wean local governments from grant dependency and to establish a sustainable connection with financial markets that municipalities could rely on in infrastructure financing. These goals consistently proved premature and ill suited to the country context.

---

[1]Municipal bank access to intergovernmental intercepts greatly facilitated loan recoveries in Brazil.

The initial results reported in table 5.1 are striking: all five Africa projects were rated as "unsatisfactory for outcome."[2] All were assessed as having low or no sustainability. All failed to meet reasonable disbursement standards; some did not disburse any funds at all. The conditions for implementing the market model were clearly not in place. Based on some of these difficult experiences with the lending model in Africa, a more gradual approach, discussed in the next chapter, evolved in some countries. Nonetheless, although this model of intermediation may be said to have been tried and to have failed in Sub-Saharan Africa, it is newly proposed from time to time.

What went wrong? The "unsatisfactory" results from using financial institutions as intermediaries and 100 percent lending as the intermediation strategy can be traced to three factors.

Local governments' borrowing capacity was overestimated. Under their existing financial conditions at the time of appraisal, none of the countries in table 5.1 had municipal sectors (or states, in the case of Nigeria) capable of repaying loans of the magnitude foreseen in the new projects. Operating surpluses, where they existed, fell short of required repayment capacity. The programs were designed around the expectation that ambitious revenue improvements would be realized, and that this transformation in local revenue capacity would permit loan repayments. Indeed, it was argued that the obligation of making loan repayments under World Bank programs would force municipal borrowers to strengthen local revenue mobilization and collection so that loans could be repaid.

Reality failed to justify this optimism. Under the revenue enhancement programs put in place in Nigeria, for example, the states of Adamawa and Tarala actually collected less than 10 percent of targeted property tax revenues. Planned increases in water tariffs did not occur. There were no surpluses in municipal or state operating accounts.

Even when credit rating agencies were brought in to assess borrowing capacity, it was overestimated. In Zimbabwe, a credit rating agency from South Africa was asked to estimate municipal borrowing capacity. It estimated that, assuming revenue-improvement action plans were implemented as deemed feasible, local governments could borrow US$25.8 million.

---

[2]Where individual components were rated, the rating refers to multisite infrastructure subproject financing.

Table 5.1. Municipal On-Lending Projects in Sub-Saharan Africa

Country	Project #	Approval fiscal year	Loan/grant	Instrument	Disbursement rate (%)[a]	Subloan repayment rate (%)	IEG outcome rating
Côte d'Ivoire	P001156	1989	All loan	Municipal development fund (MDF)	72	5.4	Unsatisfactory
Côte d'Ivoire	P037575	1995	All loan	MDF	0	n.a.	Unsatisfactory
Kenya	P001288	1983	All loan	MDF	65	20–30[b]	Unsatisfactory
Nigeria	P002099	1988	All loan	Commercial banks	0	n.a.	Unsatisfactory
Zimbabwe	P045029	1997	Loan component	MDF	3	0	Unsatisfactory

Source: Authors' calculations. See appendix 1 for further details and IEG Project Evaluation Database.

Note: n.a. not applicable.

[a]Percentage of funds disbursed under original program design.

[b]Repayment rate for all loans under Local Government Loans Authority during this period.

As events transpired, the municipalities in question in the following years were unable to cover the operating costs of their municipal services, much less provide required maintenance or service their debt. Worries that a sunset provision would be needed to wean local governments from directed credit turned out to be irrelevant. These local governments weren't ready to **start** taking directed credit responsibly.

It is true that each of these countries experienced political and financial shocks that introduced unanticipated stress in municipal finances. However, such stresses are common, and dramatic improvements in local government revenues simply are not—anywhere in the world, much less in its poorest countries. Building a municipal infrastructure lending program around the expectation of a dramatic strengthening of municipal finances in a short period is a recipe for problems. Experience in developing and industrial countries alike has shown that there are all sorts of limitations—political and social, among others—to a rapid build-up of government revenues, and that rigid adherence to an all-lending model for financially constrained municipalities is problematic, no matter how appealing the apparent incentives for financial discipline may be.

Municipal governments were unwilling to borrow when grant funds were available. The local governments involved in these programs were reluctant to borrow when other donors were providing grants. Even the apparent modest success of the Côte d'Ivoire Municipal Fund Development Project in making loans was less than it may have appeared. Five of the 19 municipal loans were used for local counterpart funding for United States Agency for International Development (USAID) grant programs, and another local loan was used to provide counterpart funding for French aid. The reluctance to borrow was pronounced, even when World Bank project preparation apparently had identified numerous specific subprojects to be financed through loans, with municipal agreement, and when other donors had agreed to channel their financing through the municipal development fund (MDF) on the same terms as the World Bank's. Ultimately donors chose grant financing for similar investments, greatly reducing the effective demand for credit.

In response to the weak demand for subloans, the Côte d'Ivoire project was revised. The targeting of small cities was dropped, and investment emphasis was switched from public good subprojects to revenue-generating subprojects that were supposed to pay for themselves, such as markets and lorry parks. Still, with grants readily available as an alternative, no borrowing demand materialized. This experience illustrates a broader phenomenon. Projects that use a borrowing model on market-oriented terms are vulnerable to the "second window" problem. Low-income countries are particularly likely to be recipients of aid on these concessional terms, and assuming that the less attractive borrowing option will be chosen has usually proven over-optimistic.

Lenders were unwilling to lend. Lenders also perceived the inherent risk in these programs. Nigerian commercial banks refused to accept the combination of subnational credit risk, foreign exchange risk, and political risk, as the original terms of the 1988 World Bank project required. All commercial banks—the intended intermediaries—declined to participate in the program.

Municipal loan repayment rates demonstrate that the perception of high risk was accurate. After more than a decade of experience, municipal loan repayment rates in the Côte d'Ivoire under the Municipal Development Project were 5.4 percent. The Local Government Loans Authority in Kenya struggled with municipal loan repayment rates of around 20 percent.

Eventually, the failure of market-based financial intermediation caused host countries and the World Bank to substitute direct lending or grant programs to subnational governments, cutting out the intermediating structure. Nigeria ended up making government loans directly to the states. Although the states retained the option of borrowing part of their counterpart funds from commercial banks at market rates, none did so. In Côte d'Ivoire, most of the project funds eventually were used by central government to finance a standard package of investment items for 61 municipalities. The standard package for all 61 municipalities consisted of

- one municipal office building
- office equipment for the new building
- a disposal site for solid waste
- one tractor and two trailers to haul solid waste

However, the story of UIF lending in Africa does not end there. As discussed below, operations in the Africa region evolved in response to these early failures. "Learning by doing" led to much more robust and suitable projects in Sub-Saharan Africa.

South Asia: Adapting the Credit Model

The experience with the "all-lending" model in Africa illustrates the caution needed in transplanting even successful models. South Asia has been more successful when the model was properly adapted to the context.

In India, World Bank involvement with the government of Tamil Nadu over several urban projects culminating in three different UIF projects illustrates how success can be achieved in difficult circumstances. After a series of projects for the city of Madras (now Chennai), the World Bank and the government of Tamil Nadu embarked on a statewide project (P009872) in FY1988. Although this project preceded by five years the 74th Constitutional Amendment Act, which started decentralization for urban local governments, the project design created a fund. The fund could lend and provide grants (up to 75 percent of project costs, depending on the circumstances of the municipality) for subprojects in municipalities in several cities in Tamil Nadu. It was established not to support formal decentralization, but out of a recognition that state-level agencies could not efficiently handle all urban infrastructure investment centrally. The credit disbursed well, and only one borrower in 94 defaulted on its loan from the fund, supported by state intercept authority.

Later the government and the World Bank agreed to a restructuring of the fund that involved investment by private equity owners (three financial intermediaries) and took the fund outside the strictures and heavy procedures of government administration. The restructured Tamil Nadu Urban Development Fund (TNUDF) was a creative public-private partnership that was still majority government owned, but could operate more rapidly and effectively than the typical government office. The second project (P050637) disbursed rapidly in the initial phases—far more rapidly than most lines of credit in India—although the grant component was reduced to 20 percent. Loan recoveries stayed well above 95 percent.

Nonetheless, in the later phases of this project, difficulties arose. World Bank funds were passed on to the intermediary from the state at a spread above the standard charges for intergovernmental borrowing in India. When the recommended spread of 300 basis points was added to the cost of funds to final beneficiaries, this resulted in a rate that was broadly in line with market rates at appraisal, thus meeting Operational Directive (OD) 8.30 criteria. To provide stability, any changes in the intergovernmental rate were passed on to the fund with a lag. In the later stages of the project, interest rates in India, as in the rest of the world, declined rapidly. The banking system became very liquid, and market spreads declined as well, making the TNUDF less attractive than other options, and disbursements declined accordingly.[3] These design issues were addressed in the third project (PO83780) by creating more pricing flexibility.

The intermediation model adopted in Tamil Nadu, while not perfect, was constructive in its context. It evolved on the basis of a well-established relationship with the government of Tamil Nadu, and the broad contours of the model were adapted to the prevailing conditions. But even such a model requires vigilance. The classic line of credit model promoted by the World Bank and followed in the TNUDF design sought to protect intermediary autonomy by ensuring a stable and profitable pricing structure. When the project started out, the final on-lending rates were reasonably competitive. The difficulties arose because all parties found it hard to adapt to the unexpected downward shift in market interest rates in the course of project implementation.

By contrast, a Bangladesh MDF (P041887), approved in 1999, sought to support decentralization but failed to generate demand for borrowing from local authorities. During supervision, it was discovered that the legal basis for municipal borrowing was questionable, and the project was converted from an all-loan program to an all-grant program. In a later municipal project in Pakistan (P049791), this issue was correctly identified during preparation, so only grants were offered from the outset.

Rethinking Support for Local Infrastructure Investment: Municipal Grants and Social Funds

The disappointing experience with lines of credit in Sub-Saharan African countries with 100 percent lending led to a change in strategy. Urban infrastructure projects were redesigned to

- Substitute grant financing of municipal subprojects for lending.
- Use access to project grants as leverage for inducing municipalities to improve financial management and as a way for central governments to rationalize the intergovernmental grant system.
- Place greater emphasis on increasing municipal revenue generation as a principal programmatic goal, supported by project technical assistance and other resources.

---

[3]Other difficulties, such as tight administrative controls on the municipalities that required approval of every subproject by the state municipal commissioner, also slowed the disbursement process.

- Require that adequate revenues be dedicated to infrastructure maintenance, in recognition of the fact that facilities built under donor
  programs often became non-functional for lack of maintenance. In
  effect, this alteration of priorities recognized that, even with enhanced
  revenue generation, many municipalities could not both maintain
  infrastructure projects and repay the costs of capital. Therefore, it
  was decided to finance capital costs through grants rather than loans
  while requiring that participating municipalities adequately fund
  maintenance.[4]

At approximately the same time that this reorientation of municipal infrastructure projects occurred, the World Bank was reexamining its
ability to reach poor communities, especially in countries going through
a difficult structural adjustment process. It decided to strengthen targeting of poor populations and poor neighborhoods. This involved the
development of a whole new product line, the social fund, with the primary purpose of reaching the poor. The fund relied on community-scale
subprojects to deliver direct benefits for poor households, often bypassing local governments or placing them in a secondary or advisory role.

Although the Urban Development UIFs started using these tools in
the 1980s, the hallmark of the social funds that emerged in the 1990s was
the emphasis on community participation in the selection, cofinancing,
and management of subprojects under the summary phrase "community-
driven development." Many of the new projects adopted a "comprehensive" approach toward urban poverty, supplementing improvement of
service delivery through community-scale investment projects with support for micro-enterprise development and small and medium enterprises. Local investment projects were seen as having the potential both
to increase access to basic services for the poor and to provide short-term
employment opportunities, by emphasizing labor-intensive projects that
would provide income-earning opportunities for low-skilled community residents. The shift to poverty-oriented grant funds in Africa was
not unique to the region. In the LAC region, where a number of the
successful earlier lending-driven funds originated, there was a significant
shift to poverty-oriented grant funds. Of 17 UIF projects approved in

---

[4]It should be noted that concerns with maintenance were not exclusive to grant programs, nor were
grant programs seen as a solution to problems with poor maintenance. Preconditions for receiving
funding in these projects often included commitments to provide funding for maintenance, reflecting a
legitimate concern that grant funding, unlike a commercial lending model, does not require borrowers
to demonstrate financial capacity.

FY1997–2006, only two of these were managed by the Urban Development sector board and used the lending model.

Municipal Grants Strategy

This evolution of the new grant approach in Africa is exemplified by the Senegal project in 1998 (see table 5.2). It was devised following a series of Agence d'Exécution de Travaux d'Intérêt Public (AGETIP) projects in Senegal (and elsewhere in the region) that operated much like the social funds. Those projects had limited institutional ambitions and focused on achieving results on the ground expeditiously and creating employment in countries suffering economic distress. When the 1998 project was prepared, the time was seen as ripe to move to a more substantial institutional agenda.

Success of the municipal grants strategy required a reasonable quid pro quo to define how grants would modify municipal and intergovernmental behavior. The strategy required identifying both (1) priorities for changes in behavior in ways that could be measured, and (2) an instrument for conveying these priorities to local governments in a manner that would capture their attention. Table 5.2 summarizes the approaches that have been taken in various country projects.

With respect to municipal performance targets, these projects (and others of similar design) emphasize own-source revenue mobilization and establishment of dedicated maintenance funds, though in some cases, in which the targets have been preceded by municipal audits that identify priority needs, the targets are more elaborate. It became common for a time for projects to require that 3 percent of local revenues be set aside for infrastructure maintenance. The rationale behind this quantitative target is obscure, and subsequent Implementation Completion Reports (ICRs) found that this level of maintenance funding was inadequate to stem serious asset deterioration.

Two instruments have been preferred for using grants to modify municipal behavior. The Urban Decentralization and Investment Project in Senegal introduced municipal contracts as a way to express mutual obligations between the central grant authority and the municipality. The process began with a municipal audit that identified priority weaknesses to be remedied in local financial and infrastructure management. The findings, with local agreement, were incorporated into a Municipal Adjustment Plan (MAP) that spelled out changes that the municipal government would carry out in exchange for receiving specified grant amounts and access to blended grant or loan financing of infrastructure projects.

Table 5.2. Municipal Grants and Infrastructure Programs

Country	Project #	Approval fiscal year	Grant/loan	Performance targets	Instrument	Community participation	IEG outcome rating
Senegal	P002365	1998	Blend, scaled by fiscal capacity	Maintenance fund at 3% of revenues; later raised to 7%. Goals for increasing own-source revenue and reducing arrears per Municipal Adjustment Plan.	Municipal contract	Not specified	Highly satisfactory
Ghana	P050624	2000	Grant	10% (real) increase in own-source revenues. Create maintenance fund at 3% of municipal revenue.	Standard project eligibility	Community role in project prioritization; community cofinancing	Satisfactory
Uganda	P077477	2003	Grant	30% increase in own-source revenue; adequate maintenance	Performance grant: (+ 20% for reaching target)	Participation in project prioritization	Active project
Georgia	P050910	1998	Loan	Targets for financial management and planning reform; own-source revenue increase	Municipal contract	Not specified	Satisfactory
Karnataka (India)	P079675	2006	Grant	Targets for own-source revenue growth and management	Performance grant	Not specified	Active project
Punjab (Pakistan)	P083929	2006	Grant	Targets for own-source revenue collection and management	Performance grant	Not specified	Active project

Source: Authors' calculations. See appendix 1 for further details and IEG Project Evaluation Database.

Two of the components of the MAP were a priority investment plan and a priority maintenance plan. Despite initial reservations, the MAPs were taken seriously by participating municipalities and the Ministry of Finance. All 67 municipal governments in Senegal signed MAP agreements. One of the features of the agreements was guaranteed regular delivery of grant amounts according to a predefined schedule. Another was monthly payments by municipalities of their obligations for matching investment funds and, later, repayment of the debt portion of financing. This kept MAP obligations at the top of municipal "to-do" lists. Senegal's record of achievement in meeting municipal targets was impressive; the project was rated "highly satisfactory."

Some important features driving success in the Senegal model are noteworthy. First, considerable time was taken during preparation to develop all the tools needed to implement this approach and to identify and train local consultants who could help municipalities use these tools, thus economizing the delays inherent in this sort of preconditionality. Second, the model used in this contract was adopted by all the donors active in the country and mainstreamed by the Ministry of Finance in its dealings with municipalities in Senegal. This type of mainstreaming may not be feasible or acceptable in all countries, but it is clear that in countries where international funds played such an important role, it was instrumental in making a fairly demanding approach work.

The municipal contract approach was subsequently employed in a number of other countries in Africa, as well as in Georgia (P050910), in FY1998. The results in Georgia are instructive because they offer a dramatic contrast with Senegal. The project was prepared in record time, about four months,[5] in a country that had little familiarity with the World Bank and that had recently experienced a dramatic economic downturn estimated at 55 percent of gross domestic product (GDP). Municipalities in Georgia never accepted that the contracts between local and central government had the force of law and did not fulfill their contractual obligations. This development was not altogether surprising given the recent dramatic economic and political transition experienced in the country. Moreover, Georgia's program financed 40 percent of the cost of subprojects through loans with 15 percent interest rates,[6] and municipalities had to finance 20 percent of the costs themselves. This greatly dampened the incentives for municipalities in straitened circumstances to modify financial management.

---

[5]The IDA timetable appears to have played a role.

[6]Forty percent was also provided through grants, and 20 percent was to come from local government contributions. The inflation rate in 1996 was about 14 percent.

When the first project was prepared, the central government hoped to make municipalities financially independent, and the loan program was seen as a means of accelerating this process. At the same time, rather than allowing municipalities to choose to borrow, the government also wanted to direct investments to the areas of its choice. The hope of promoting financial discipline proved unrealistic given the lack of a supporting framework to encourage a lending culture, and the loan recoveries suffered. Bad loans eventually reached 25 percent of the total portfolio.

The Georgia case is instructive in illustrating the scope for a turnaround. In the course of project implementation, the country experienced the Rose Revolution, which had a significant impact on intergovernmental relations, among others. The government took a number of steps to put in place a framework that supported local government borrowing and changed its behavior toward local governments that did not service their debt. Bad loans in the portfolio have fallen by two orders of magnitude and now stand at 0.25 percent. The difficult environment in Georgia was poorly suited to the lending and municipal contract model that underpinned the design of the first World Bank project, but government decisions after the Rose Revolution have had a positive impact on what were unsatisfactory results.

The second instrument of enforcement that has gained favor is the performance grant. Such grants have been built into an increasing proportion of municipal infrastructure projects and typically stipulate that municipalities will become eligible for additional grant amounts or will become eligible to enter the grant program if they meet certain standards. Most often, performance is measured in terms of own-source revenue mobilization, or revenue collection rates, in the first instance, but the performance conditions are designed to expand into other areas of financial management and service delivery performance in later stages. In addition to attempting to modify local government behavior, performance grants are intended to have a demonstration effect on central authorities and to encourage an overhaul of the intergovernmental grant system to strengthen its performance incentives.

The jury is still out on the effectiveness of performance grants as an implementing device. Follow-up monitoring of whether grants actually were increased for municipalities that met performance targets and lowered (or eliminated) for municipalities that failed to meet targets has been weak. There are strong political pressures to give equal regional coverage in World Bank–supported municipal grant programs and not to penalize municipalities that fail to meet performance targets. Whether performance grants, where implemented as designed, have sustainably changed municipal behavior in significant ways also is unclear. **Systematic evaluation of the most recent generation of performance grants would add greatly to an understanding of urban programs' effectiveness.**

Supporting Municipal Infrastructure Investment in Centralized Systems

World Bank programs supporting local infrastructure investment are often seen as support for a significant move toward decentralization. However, some countries maintain a unitary system of government, in which local infrastructure priorities are determined largely as part of intergovernmental capital planning organized from above. Financing is extended to local authorities through centralized governmental financial institutions. In many other cases, decentralization, while formally declared, has often progressed very little, and the near future promises, at most, gradual further decentralization. Yet decentralized investment needs are significant. What is a reasonable set of institutional objectives in this environment?

Experience in Morocco illustrates the issues involved. The Fonds d'Equipement Communal (FEC) was modeled after Crédit Local de France.[7] Up to a point, the FEC has followed a parallel path of reform. In the 1990s, it was transformed from a government agency into a publicly owned, specialized financial institution and subsequently into a full-fledged bank supervised by the Central Bank.

By many standards, FEC is an efficient institution. It raises its own financing through bond issues and other forms of borrowing at five- to seven-year tenures. Although this does not eliminate term intermediation risk (FEC lends for up to 15-year periods), it places FEC at the upper end of responsibly self-financed municipal intermediaries. In the past, FEC borrowed with a government guarantee. The government has now terminated guarantees for FEC borrowing. On international loans, FEC absorbs foreign exchange risk on its own without government participation. Morocco's legal framework was modified to allow competition from private financial institutions in the market for municipal lending. At the same time, as an on-lender, FEC has been able to widen its positive net intermediation spread to 2.6 percent and substantially reduce its administrative costs.

---

[7] Box 4.1 provides background on the history of the Crédit Local de France.

Under the World Bank's Second Municipal Finance Project, FEC managed a US$150 million line of credit used to finance 210 municipal subprojects. More than three-quarters were targeted to cities with populations of fewer than 150,000, and more than three-quarters were targeted to basic infrastructure services. All physical investment targets were met or exceeded.

Nonetheless, for two years this project was rated "unsatisfactory." In the final ICR, borrower performance was still rated "unsatisfactory." The reasons for this rating seem to reflect the expectation that FEC would fully replicate Crédit Local de France's reform path. The government failed to privatize FEC as a joint stock company, the final step it had committed to in project design. The ICR also criticized the government for not transferring full capacity for local infrastructure planning to local governments and remarked (critically) that the process of investment planning did not allow the World Bank to participate in project preparation.

These may be failures with respect to the project's stated goals, but they raise the question of whether those project goals were appropriate. First, should the World Bank require decentralization as a condition of its loans? Or can it accommodate a system in which (1) municipal investment priorities are set by a centrally guided, intergovernmental planning system that identifies priorities for local coverage of basic services; (2) investments are implemented efficiently according to this intergovernmental plan; and (3) a specialized governmental finance institution, operating at its own credit risk and taking responsibility for raising finance on the domestic market, on-lends to local authorities to finance subproject investments? Second, should the World Bank consider it a failure that FEC did not follow the path of corporatization and privatization that France achieved only a few years earlier? Is there strong reason to believe that the failure to launch an initial public offering (IPO) of FEC shares compromised the development impact of this project materially, given the state of both decentralization and financial markets in Morocco?

The case of FEC also raises the question of consistency among the different objectives embodied in one project. The Project Appraisal Document (PAD) raised the concern that privileged access to funding for the FEC was preventing other private intermediaries from lending to municipalities. Project conditionality accordingly foresaw an IPO, following on an opening up to competition from other lenders. At the same time, FEC was obliged to meet project-specific targets for directing lending to poorer municipalities. These targets did not apply to the private competitors, whose entry in market the World Bank had encouraged.

The above situation is not unique to Morocco. The Caisse des Prêts et de Soutien aux Collectivités Locales (CPSCL) in Tunisia encountered similar difficulties with World Bank conditions. It completed its municipal infrastructure investment plan, as agreed with the World Bank, 16 months ahead of schedule, but the project was criticized for lack of decentralization to local governments and for failing to privatize the financial intermediary. Because government revenues were not devolved to municipalities as hoped for at appraisal, the municipalities became overextended as they borrowed as envisaged in the central plan. This posed certain risks to the municipal fund, but the issue was eventually brought to the attention of the government and resolved, thanks to the efforts of both the CPSCL and the World Bank. This situation underscored the necessary dependence of the municipal fund on government's good will in such a centralized environment, conflicting with the arguably unrealistic model of autonomy and market orientation pursued under the project. But that dependence does not negate the efficient services the municipal fund provided in helping the local governments turn plan allocations for priority investments into viable local projects.

In the Tamil Nadu project discussed earlier, attracting substantial additional finance from the three financial institutions that were the original private equity holders in the TNUDF was considered an important feature of the original project design. Progress on this score was the subject of dated covenants in the loan documents. This emphasis on asking for additional exposure from the original TNUDF private sponsors in the project design, although understandable given the willingness of three investors to make nominal capital contributions at the establishment of the fund, was excessive given the status of decentralization. Although Tamil Nadu had decentralized more than most Indian states, the administrative and financial autonomy of the urban local governments was so limited that each subproject still needed to be approved by the state. Local governments' capacity to borrow was limited by a narrow and inflexible revenue base, the parameters of which were controlled by the state.[8] These conditions, coupled with a less favorable tax treatment of dividends than expected at appraisal, dampened the enthusiasm of the private stakeholders for further investments. Fortunately, the supervision team and government worked together to find an alternative means of meeting the spirit of the covenants. Even though the problem was successfully resolved in the end, in retrospect, the emphasis on

---

[8]For example, the state imposed a moratorium on property revaluation for the entire period of the project.

mobilizing private finance probably distracted attention from the simple, but valuable, function the fund performed in helping local governments work out investment programs they could afford and manage.

These three cases suggest that the World Bank may be overlooking genuine opportunities for value addition in a rush to meet broad corporate objectives, such as private participation, before the time is ripe. In a highly centralized environment, a good, simple model of investment finance for local governments has considerable value. Artificially accelerating access to private markets may compromise realistic short-term objectives without doing much to achieve the ultimate goal of private access. It seems arbitrary to insist on these objectives in all UIFs in the absence of empirical evidence that decentralization or rapid privatization of financial intermediaries has consistently yielded superior outcomes, as judged either by infrastructure service quality or by citizen satisfaction.

Commercial Banks and the Development of Sustainable Municipal Credit Systems

Commercial banks dominate the financial landscape of most middle-income countries (MICs). They are the primary institutions for mobilizing savings and the primary lenders. Many World Bank projects in MICs have as a development objective the establishment of sustainable municipal credit markets—either from the outset or in the future. Municipalities would be able to borrow, when needed, at market rates for longer-term tenures to finance part of their infrastructure investments.

In view of this common objective, and of the dominant financial role that commercial banks occupy, it is surprising that more World Bank programs have not operated through commercial banks as the ultimate lenders to municipalities. More often, projects have established new funds, operating outside the existing institutional structure, to be lending vehicles to municipalities. Yet there is a track record of experience that suggests that working with existing institutions can be made to work in the correct circumstances.

Four World Bank projects that have had credit market development as a principal development objective are illustrative.

In an FY 1991 project in Colombia (P006861),[9] the World Bank supported a recently restructured apex fund, Financiera de Desarrollo Ter-

---

[9]A follow-on project in FY1998 is one of only two urban development UIFs approved in the FY1997–FY2006 period in LAC.

ritorial Sociedad Anonyma (FINDETER), a second-tier refinancing agent for commercial banks that made loans to municipalities and municipal utilities. FINDETER took term transformation risk, but commercial banks were required to evaluate and assume municipal credit risk, and they were allowed to price their product accordingly, subject to a cap on spreads established by government that was considerably higher than the rates prevailing under the old administered system.

The predecessor to FINDETER had a long history as a financing source for Colombia's municipal investments and had well-established relationships with commercial banks as the retail agents in municipal lending. The support of the World Bank and Inter-American Development Bank (IADB) allowed FINDETER to shift to a more market-oriented model and to reorganize itself as a leaner, more agile, and faster-acting institution that had a clear role to play in supporting commercial bank lending. International financial institution (IFI) support also helped FINDETER and municipal lending come through Colombia's financial crisis in the late 1990s. The FINDETER model is characterized by incremental change shifting to a stronger market orientation as the decentralization process (eight years old when the first project was introduced) moved forward.

In another project (P056192), in Bosnia and Herzegovina in FY1999, the World Bank succeeded in introducing commercial banks to the municipal sector. The project provided a line of credit to participating commercial banks for municipal lending, as well as joint technical assistance to banks and municipalities, to establish common expectations regarding creditworthiness standards. Eight banks formally participated in the project as municipal lenders through the project's line of credit. Other commercial banks participated in the project's training and opened municipal lending as a line of business activity, drawing solely on their own resources. Compliance with World Bank safeguards was handled by a project unit in the Ministry of Finance, not the participating commercial banks. This project established a reliable municipal credit market through commercial banks, although it took a while for the model to catch on, and disbursements of the World Bank funds did not materialize for two years. By the end of the project, banks were competing for the business and bidding down spreads. In spite of this success, continuation of this type of borrowing is now at risk because of an International Monetary Fund (IMF) agreement that does not permit subnational borrowing, except in association with international donor programs.

In a project in Poland (P035082), the World Bank also sought to provide a line of credit for commercial banks. However, it negotiated the design of its project for three years prior to approval, in FY1998. Originally the project was to operate through a newly created municipal development fund. Later, this approach was dropped in favor of a design that created a line of credit made available to two participating commercial banks, identified at appraisal, for on-lending to municipalities.

Possibly out of concern for rigorous application of on-lender eligibility requirements, the project offered no flexibility for other banks to opt in during project implementation, although the municipal lending market proved to be very dynamic. The project progressed slowly, and the World Bank's many auxiliary safeguard requirements were perceived as burdensome for the two participating banks. During the project's lifetime, Poland's municipal credit market exploded in magnitude and became a reliable source of financing for local governments. Commercial banks commonly extended their loan tenures to municipal governments to 10 years, or even longer for major infrastructure systems. However, the project did little to contribute to development of this successful market. Commercial banks found it simpler to deal with municipalities directly, without the intermediation of the World Bank. One of the two commercial banks involved canceled its participation in the project before making a loan. In total, less than 10 percent of budgeted on-lending through the project took place.

In Lithuania in FY1999, the World Bank did move to establish an MDF (P035802) to on-lend to municipal governments, bypassing the commercial bank structure. But as in Poland, commercial bank lending to municipalities grew on its own, while availability of grant funding increased rapidly with accession to the European Union. Banks preferred to deal directly with municipalities on loans rather than be associated with the MDF. Other donors such as the European Investment Bank (EIB) came forward with competing credit lines at more attractive terms. Lithuania quickly developed a reliable municipal credit market in which creditworthy municipalities could obtain financing from commercial banks at interest rates and tenures comparable to what the MDF was offering—and without many of the additional requirements for safeguards and procurement rules. At project closing, the MDF had disbursed only a small portion of the funds budgeted for on-lending.

This example illustrates a key vulnerability of a separate municipal fund structure or unduly rigid eligibility arrangements for participating on-lenders. Although an MDF may be just what's needed in environments where other lenders are not likely to come forward, if there are other options the separate MDF runs the risk of offering a product that is not competitive over time.

The experiences in Poland and Lithuania signal issues that are in some ways specific to these transition economy markets with particularly strong commercial banking sectors and relatively well-endowed municipalities. But these experiences are also an indicator of the burden that World Bank safeguards impose on the ultimate objective of a transition to the full market access model. If the World Bank product is not competitive when there are alternative lenders, then it is important to ask how the World Bank's procedures affect the evolution toward a less exclusive, directed system. The World Bank may be slowing the achievement of the final objective of full market access by providing privileged access to capital while imposing burdensome requirements that the market would not.

Some basic lessons can be learned from these experiences.

Credit Risk

The essential element of a commercial bank program is that the commercial banks accept credit risk. This forces private sector lenders with money at risk to develop appraisal methodologies that assess municipal creditworthiness and subproject risk, the critical elements of a sustainable system. This model requires that municipalities, by managing their own affairs well, have the means to be reasonable risks. Only a subset of the subnational markets in developing countries is suited to this model. One of the lessons learned is that this subset is not nearly as large as "decentralization" efforts may suggest. The art of project design lies in determining when these conditions pertain and how to adapt when they do not.

Foreign Exchange Risk

Municipal lending is most appropriately done in local currency. Municipal governments do not have opportunities to earn foreign exchange and rarely have access to hedging instruments that make it prudent to take on debts denominated in foreign currency. The handling of foreign exchange risk is a key issue in the design of any municipal lending program supported by international donors. If the risk is absorbed by government without cost to the borrowers, a significant and uncertain subsidy is introduced into the system. Such a subsidy may be appropriate in lower-income countries, but in middle-income countries on the verge of introducing their own markets, it is a distorting factor. Poland introduced a national law that prohibited municipal borrowing in foreign currency. The law delayed disbursements of the World Bank project funds for 18 months until a government waiver was obtained for the project. When a swap market in the currency exists, the World Bank can offer low-cost swaps into local currency.[10] When that option is not available, charging a reasonable premium for foreign exchange risk is likely to be a better solution than simply pushing this risk onto local governments.

Open Commercial Bank Participation

Selecting only two participating commercial banks delayed implementation of the project in Poland greatly and ultimately undermined the project's impact. It is impossible to foresee accurately how vigorously a given commercial bank will pursue program participation. A preferable design is to establish clear criteria for participation (in terms of banks' capital adequacy, audit and loan recovery record, and municipal lending preparation), then accept as many banks as meet the criteria and want to join the program. This design also injects an element of bank competition into the program that speeds disbursement and provides more options for participating municipalities. As noted, eight banks participated in the Bosnia project, some of which, after initial enrollment, were bought out by Austrian banks with greater familiarity with municipal lending. A Czech project supported by USAID introduced 11 banks to municipal lending with the express goal of establishing a strong competitive market in the municipal sector.

---

[10]The currencies in which the World Bank can offer swaps as of January 2008, are listed in appendix 3.

CHAPTER 6

Agenda for Future Work

This analysis has demonstrated that the use of urban infrastructure funds (UIFs) has declined just as demographic changes are creating demands for urban infrastructure in a host of secondary cities and towns. Democratization and decentralization mean that ever-increasing numbers of elected municipal governments are charged with meeting these demands, even if only to a partial extent. Reaching large numbers of far-flung cities and towns and their elected governments is difficult, both for governments and international financial institutions, without the help of local partners in appropriate institutional arrangements. UIFs are designed to perform this function, and reinvigorating the World Bank's work with UIFs will position the World Bank better to meet the emerging development needs of its clients.

This initiative to rebuild the UIF business line rests on a solid foundation of good project performance, as measured by the World Bank's independent evaluations by the Independent Evaluation Gropu (IEG). A number of models have emerged that work in a variety of circumstances. But the lessons learned from experience also indicate an important substantive agenda not only for undertaking more of these projects but also for doing them better and tailoring them to emerging needs.

The agenda for future work has two important dimensions: operational and research. The operational dimension should focus on implementation issues that will be of importance in future projects. Several issues are emerging as key to project design in a new generation of UIF projects. These issues come in the form of questions, rather than a set of design parameters. These questions should be addressed in project design in a manner that meets broad project objectives and fits country circumstances.

Operational Challenges for the Future:
1) Creating an Appropriate Distance between Central Government
and Municipalities (Sovereign Guarantee and Foreign Exchange Risk).
Increasingly, national governments wish to encourage fiscal discipline
in local governments as they are held to tighter standards themselves
and their direct control of local government finances diminishes. Still,
national governments retain a role in providing support and investment
funding to local governments, in part because their ability to raise revenue efficiently is superior. The issue of fiscal discipline in a decentralized
context is one that lends itself to steady adaptation, even fine-tuning
rather than a single discrete reform. The tension between budgetary discipline and decentralization of investment decisions and responsibilities
is structural in all but the most centralized and authoritarian unitary
governments. In addition, as the state of the financial sector evolves, this
too can imply changes in the sorts of arrangements suitable for facilitat-
ing municipal access to capital finance.

World Bank projects targeting local governments necessarily touch on
these sensitive areas because they involve passing external funds from
central governments to lower levels. Project design must avoid disrupt-
ing the arrangements currently in place, and sometimes it can help to
improve them. Accordingly, transplanting successful models from other
countries is fraught with risks. Achieving the right balance demands very
specific tailoring to individual countries' circumstances with regard to
the intergovernmental finance dimension.

**Ensuring that a UIF is not disruptive to intergovernmental relations
nearly always involves being explicit about matters such as foreign
exchange risk.** It is usually unrealistic to ask municipalities or UIFs to
bear the foreign exchange risk, because they have very little capacity
to hedge, and, unlike central governments, they don't earn in foreign
exchange. **There are several means of addressing this problem; which
one works best for the client will vary from country to country.** The
central government (or provincial government in some federal systems)
can take the foreign exchange risk and pass along a projected annual cost
equivalent to the borrower. Not charging for foreign exchange risk is not
recommended when funds are on-lent, because this provides an implicit
and opaque subsidy that can be handled better otherwise. However,
some governments handle arrangements for passing all intergovernmental funds according to a specific formula. It is rarely a good idea to request
changes in such a formula for a specific project unless it is dramatically
ill suited to project needs. The International Bank for Reconstruction and

Development (IBRD) also now offers swaps at very low cost for a number of currencies, thereby providing the option of avoiding the foreign exchange risk altogether for a very modest cost.[1]

Some governments are reluctant to offer the sovereign guarantee required by the World Bank and other international financial institutions (IFIs) for debts incurred by local governments. UIF projects actually make it easier to avoid providing such guarantees, because World Bank funds are passed on to an intermediary rather than directly to local governments. The intermediary, rather than the municipality, thus benefits from the sovereign guarantee. When the government no longer wishes to extend a sovereign guarantee for intermediaries borrowing from the IFIs, as is the case for Fonds d'Equipement Communal (FEC) in Morocco, the World Bank Group subnational facility managed out of the International Finance Corporation (IFC) could be accessed, since it does not require a sovereign guarantee. So a number of options are available to address this issue for UIFs. It is also important to note, however, that both foreign exchange risk and sovereign guarantee are not significant issues when project funds are passed through on a grant basis.

2) Responding to the Diverse Needs and Capacities of Municipalities within a Single Country

This review has shown that it is very difficult to combine a large number of objectives in a single UIF project. **It is particularly difficult to use one intermediation model to meet the investment needs of all municipalities, especially in a large and diverse province or country.** Specialized intermediaries operating on a credit model will tend to lend to larger and stronger municipalities, often concentrating a good deal of their portfolios in the political capital or commercial center of a country, and will gravitate to revenue-generating projects rather than basic infrastructure. That outcome is the logical result of using the credit model, especially when the financial sector is liberalizing and there is competition among financial service providers.

Smaller municipalities are less likely to want to incur debts, and they will not be particularly attractive clients for commercially oriented institutions, as has been amply demonstrated in project experience. If reaching smaller cities and towns is the objective, projects will need to focus on designing good grant programs or offering a combination of grants and loans. Providing grants on only a performance basis will necessarily leave

---

[1]The currencies in which the World Bank can offer swaps as of January 2008 are listed in appendix 3.

out the relatively poorly performing municipalities, especially if funds are distributed following a competitive model.[2] The specific objectives for decentralized finance should dictate project design; UIF projects that target smaller cities and towns can be poorly suited to pursuing more complex sectoral goals or corporate objectives like Public-Private Partnership (PPP). **Often more than one type of operation will be needed to meet the variety of needs in a given country.** For example, in the Punjab in Pakistan, an FY2006 UIF project (P083929) offered grants to municipalities with some performance elements. Now the World Bank is preparing a Development Policy Loan (DPL) that covers the needs of the province's largest cities, excluded from the UIF, and addresses important policy issues on intergovernmental relations and the framework for municipal finance.

3) Measuring Results with More Rigor and Precision
Measuring results can be particularly challenging in UIF projects. Because individual subprojects are purposely small and are not all identified prior to approval of the World Bank project, the approach used for a standard investment loan is not directly applicable. Nonetheless, results must be measured with rigor if rebuilding this business line is to achieve the desired results. There are two key issues in measuring project results: the quality and sustainability of the subprojects and the impact of the UIF on overall access to capital funding for municipalities in the target country or province.

a. Selection Criteria for Subprojects: Assuring Quality and Sustainability
In a fund project, one of the most important functions the World Bank delegates is subproject selection. Over the years, the World Bank's appraisal process for standard investment projects has honed a strong capacity to identify white elephants. Explicit attention should now be turned to helping local agents perform this same function effectively— not because there is evidence that funds perform this function poorly, but because current processes generate little evidence one way or the other. More explicit attention needs to be focused on the design of the selection process and assessment of the results it has achieved in appraisal, supervision, and evaluation.

World Bank practice regarding selection criteria has changed over the years. Traditional fund projects emphasized economic analysis, although

---

[2]Zinnes (forthcoming) discusses a number of competitive models in public policy, including performance grants.

cost-effectiveness analysis is often preferred to economic rates of return (ERRs), and rarely are these examined after the subproject is completed. The Levy Report correctly pointed out that private intermediaries rarely calculate ERRs and that it was inappropriate to burden lines of credit with this computation, except for very large subprojects. When an intermediary must compete in capital markets for funds and show profitability, incentives are properly aligned to select viable projects most of the time.

However, as has been argued earlier, much decentralized finance in developing countries, including in World Bank projects, will continue to involve elements of subsidy provided through public sector channels. In such cases, the government, on behalf of the taxpayer, should assess whether public monies have been used well or wasted.

In fund-type projects, it is quite rare to find mention in Implementation Completion Reports (ICRs) of ex-post economic or financial assessment of a subproject.[3] In the "social fund" type projects, community participation was seen as sufficient to guarantee that the projects selected were the right investments. Cost-effectiveness analysis was used to assess whether, ex-post, the fund's projects had been more costly than those built by other agencies, such as the water authority or the education ministry. Many ICRs cite community surveys measuring satisfaction with the projects selected. All of this information is useful, but it doesn't provide much comfort that projects are well designed and executed, can be built at close to projected costs, and can actually provide the benefits expected. For example, are the household wastewater connections made so that consumers actually benefit from the processing facility?[4] Are facilities adequately maintained so that they are still functioning five years after construction? Projects should be designed to encourage UIFs to undertake these assessments regularly, report on them in the course of supervision, and use the information to improve their own subproject selection practices.

Although traditional ERR analysis has fallen out of favor for a variety of reasons, a simple ERR analysis has the merit of requiring explicit assumptions about key project features such as cost, time to completion,

---

[3] About 85 percent of UD sector board UIF projects use ERRs at appraisal, and 60 percent of Rural Development's (RDV) UIF projects do so; less than 20 percent of SP UIF projects use ERRs. In a subsample of more than 40 percent completed projects across all sector boards, only a few reviewed ERRs ex-post. A somewhat higher number of SP projects examined cost-effectiveness analysis.

[4] Impact evaluation research on community-driven projects has shown that often community expectations are so low that they do not enforce reasonable standards (Banerjee 2007). Also, strategic behavior in the presence of grants can skew community responses to questionnaires (OED 2002). As such, measures of community satisfaction alone cannot be relied on to ensure that subprojects have been executed effectively.

and economic lifetime of assets created. These assumptions can be tested for plausibility up front and validated after completion of the subproject to determine whether the expected economic benefit was actually realized. If ERR analysis is considered too burdensome, then other tests of reasonableness that can be applied ex-ante and ex-post should be used. The issue is not the specifics of the methodology; it is much more the need for a consistent and robust measure for identifying badly designed projects and failures. This is particularly pertinent when subsidies of any kind are involved, because the incentives for waste, political influence, and corruption are greater when there is not even a modest financial cost to the recipient.[5] Many funds probably already perform this kind of evaluation to some extent, and it would be worthwhile to invest in learning more about effective project selection practices at the fund level.

b. The Role of UIFs within Aggregate Financing of Municipal Infrastructure

Nearly all UIF projects seek not only to improve the quality of investments in urban infrastructure, as just discussed, but also to change the aggregate pattern of municipal infrastructure financing. A typical project document asserts that, given pressure on national government budgets, a lesser share of central spending can be expected to be devoted to investment at the local level or that local investment can be increased for the same level of central expenditure. UIF lending should (1) increase the share of municipal investment financed by borrowing, (2) substitute to some degree for state grants and subsidies in financing local investment, and (3) help boost aggregate municipal capital investment or help sustain prior investment levels in the face of budgetary pressures. Projects intended to develop municipal credit markets will have further goals, such as creating a sustainable, competitive private market in municipal lending.

Goals such as these typically provide the primary development rationale for introducing UIFs. Yet it is rare for projects to assess the sources of capital finance that local governments are tapping prior to a project's commencement or to monitor how the aggregate financing mix and aggregate investment level change during project implementation.[6] **An**

---

[5]It is a separate question, as yet unanswered empirically, whether funds on-lent at market cost actually provided tangible additional incentives for selecting good projects.

[6]The review of more than forty recently closed projects turned up no cases in which the ICR cited figures of incremental capital finance in evaluating outcomes and results. In some cases, it appears that such claims could be made, and that the information might be available, but the evaluation discussion did not marshal data or provide an analytical framework to do so.

essential part of project design and evaluation should be to assess the sources of funds being used for urban infrastructure investment prior to the project, to identify the role the project is intended to play in improving access to financing, and to monitor outcomes, not just for funds the UIF disburses, but for aggregate financing of local capital investment.

Such analysis helps in selecting appropriate intermediaries and onlending terms at the outset of project preparation. As the discussion in chapter 5 showed, when certain projects failed, the design had not taken into account all the different sources of finance to municipalities.

Such analysis also is essential for evaluating project impact, for identifying when the intermediation model for local governments needs to be modified, and for determining whether more or less IFI involvement is needed. No successful model of municipal intermediation can work forever in changing circumstances. Continual assessment of market development should become a building block of project design. How to focus these assessments best will vary from country to country, depending on the way municipal infrastructure is financed and on the policy objectives of a project. Box 6.1 offers the example of market monitoring and assessment carried out as part of a UIF intermediary project in the Czech Republic, supported by USAID.

4) Treating Subsidies for Urban Infrastructure More Flexibly and Explicitly in UIFs

This review of operations showed that UIFs vary considerably with regard to the use of subsidies (typically in the form of passing on funds on a grant basis). Practices differ considerably across sector boards in the use and targeting of subsidies. The Rural Development and Social Protection sector board projects offer grants (full subsidies) in their projects. At the other extreme, private sector and financial development groups offer loans only, while the Urban Development sector board is the only one spanning both approaches in its projects. Grants have been handled in many ways, from geographical targeting of poor municipalities to participatory project selection, to across-the-board blending of all loans at "market" rates, with a fixed grant component to make the package more affordable.

Subsidies and grants can benefit from more explicit attention for a number of reasons. First, experience shows that, if anything, projects have tended to overestimate the scope for borrowing, particularly in secondary cities and towns. Second, borrowing capacity in secondary cities and towns will be limited for some time to come. Relying on loans at market

Box 6.1

Monitoring Municipal Financial Market Development: The Czech Republic

The Municipal Infrastructure Finance Company (MUFIS) was an urban infrastructure finance intermediary created by the Czech Republic under a United States Agency for International Development (USAID) assistance program to facilitate development of the municipal credit market. The goals of the project were (1) to help establish a competitive private market for municipal lending, (2) to increase the use of credit in financing municipal infrastructure investments in a responsible manner, (3) to increase the tenor of loans and other forms of credit offered to municipalities through the market, and (4) to help sustain municipal investment levels during a transition period when it was believed that central subsidies for municipal investment would decline. MUFIS operated as a second-tier financing institution that on-lent funds to qualifying commercial banks, which in turn lent to municipalities. The commercial banks assumed all credit risk and performed all credit analysis. At the same time MUFIS was introducing commercial banks to municipal lending, the technical assistance elements of the program worked with municipalities to assess their own borrowing capacity and to test a nascent municipal bond market so as to compare borrowing costs via bond issues with the costs of bank loans.

Because the goals of the project concerned overall market development, a monitoring system was created that reported quarterly on development of the capital financing market for municipalities. Monitoring results are illustrated below for 1996, the third year of the project, which began in 1994.

Item	1993 (base year)	1996
Number of banks lending to municipalities	1	8
Percentage long-term loans (4+ years)	27%	80%
Municipal bank loans outstanding (Kc)	2.5 billion	13.5 billion
Municipal bonds outstanding (Kc)	0	13.2 billion
Long-term borrowing as a percentage of municipal investment	6.8%	22.6%
State grants or subsidy as a percentage of municipal investment	23.6%	21.9%
Municipal own-source revenue as a percentage of municipal investment	69.6%	55.5%
Investment share of municipal budget	36.8%	40.4%

These measures confirmed that a highly competitive market in municipal credit was developing rapidly. The role that MUFIS and the USAID program played in this development is open to interpretation. MUFIS' share of the commercial bank lending market never exceeded 17 percent. However, all seven banks that entered the market to compete with the former State Savings Bank did so initially through MUFIS's intermediation. All Czech cities having populations in excess of 100,000 issued at least one municipal bond, and all of these cities except Prague developed their bond issue in conjunction with USAID technical assistance.

As the Czech municipal credit market matured, the MUFIS program was re-evaluated. Bank loans proved more cost-effective than municipal bonds for all except the largest municipalities and became a larger share of new borrowing by municipalities. Commercial banks began lending from their own resources, rather than accessing credit lines at MUFIS. The banks extended loan terms to 12 years. Nonperforming loans in the municipal sector as a whole never exceeded 2.5 percent. The municipal sector was assigned the lowest risk rating, after national government debt, by the Czech National Bank. In view of this successful transition, MUFIS stopped making new loans to commercial banks in 1999 and was dissolved in 2003, 10 years after its creation, with its external loans repaid.

Can monitoring of this type be carried out in other countries at a reasonable cost? Even in the 1990s, the Czech Republic benefited from municipal budget data collection not available in many countries, so equally complete monitoring often is not feasible. However, project preparation should specify what is known about the overall sources of finance for municipal infrastructure investment at baseline, what key parameters can be measured for change as the project progresses, and in what direction these parameters should be moving if the project is successful. Monitoring costs can be reduced as part of project design. In the case of the Czech Republic, the Ministry of Finance (MoF) was a project partner and shared the goal of opening up the municipal credit market. Monitoring benchmarks were agreed to with MoF at the outset, and an office for local government finance within MoF expedited release of data from government sources (including the central bank) that otherwise were not publicly available. The first round of monitoring reports was prepared by international consultants; thereafter, local consultants followed the same template.

rates will exclude a number of municipalities. Third, environmental issues from global warming to avian flu involve significant interjurisdictional spillovers deriving from economic activities in cities. The preferred economic instruments to address such issues are tax and subsidy regimes, and governments will be pressed to innovate in these areas. In fact, in some respects, the World Bank's position on cost recovery in many UIFs through market rate loans has been more strict than actual practice in highly developed countries, where mixed grant and loan financing is common for such local investments as wastewater collection and treatment or urban road construction and maintenance.

From a pragmatic and developmental perspective, a more proactive approach to subsidies is needed. The starting point should be to recognize that it is quite likely that governments already provide, in some form, capital grants to these municipalities. **Projects that work with governments to make such programs more effective can be very valuable. There are many circumstances in which an IFI is well placed to help governments work out these issues, and then provide follow-up financing.**

There are many entry points for improving subsidy programs. Often, clarifying objectives and matching them with financing availability on a sustainable basis is a sound starting point. From there, guiding principles for reform can use basic public finance concepts: economic efficiency, targeting, and administrative ease and transparency. Economic efficiency of subsidies evaluates the value of what is transferred to beneficiaries in relation to its resource cost. Targeting examines how well the target group is covered by the subsidy and how much of the subsidy leaks to nontarget groups. Administrative ease and transparency measure the level of effort and resources needed to operate the program as designed and the capacity to monitor. Where development of municipal capital markets is part of the policy objective, subsidy programs also can be evaluated from the perspective of whether they are compatible with accessing private-market capital or whether they distort or preempt that process.

5) Designing Funds that Are User Friendly to Municipal Borrowers and that Make It Easy for Financiers to "Crowd In" with Additional Finance

Over the course of the World Bank's long involvement in UIF projects, the borrowers and the supporting environments have changed considerably. Whereas in the 1970s most local government beneficiaries had little autonomy, were rarely elected, and had little choice but to accept the investment menu offered by the central government through a fund project, in many countries this has changed considerably. Even if decentralization is often incomplete, once local governments are elected, they have little choice but to be mindful of the political cycle. Financial liberalization has not opened the floodgates of finance for most municipalities. But municipalities now have more financing choices, and the financial intermediaries supported by IFIs have more competitors and market pressures than before. This does not mean that well-designed external projects have no role. Much of the above discussion has illustrated areas where IFI projects can bring value in spite of these changes. However, these shifts in the operating environment do imply that there are limits to the burdens and special procedures that external projects can continue to impose constructively.

For example, donor-imposed safeguards on the environment, relocation, and procurement are a particularly heavy burden to intermediaries trying to compete with financing sources that do not face these obligations. They also slow subproject processing, weakening the appeal to elected local governments. Because funds specialize in smaller subprojects, they aim to reach those clients least likely to have the capacity to follow these procedures, and they impose the heaviest costs. UIF projects are increasingly challenged to offer the flexibility that their clients require, just as IFIs like the World Bank have tightened and codified safeguard policies.

Some individual projects have been very creative, but there are clear signs of stress. If they are to become significant in the future, UIF projects should look for solutions that rely on country systems for safeguards, already being piloted in the World Bank. The best solution is for safeguard rules to address the issue at hand substantively and to apply equally to all local investments, not merely those having the UIF as a source of finance. UIFs should be promising candidates for piloting the application of new country systems. Many of the changes discussed above, such as democratization and decentralization, make externally imposed procedures and safeguards more burdensome; however, they also generate local demand for well-defined, practical processes to address environmental, social, and fiduciary issues for all municipal investments, regardless of the source of finance. Tailoring safeguards to work well with country systems can be an area where efforts for the World Bank to scale up its involvement in UIFs would have a strong synergy with positive local developments.

Areas for Further Analysis and Research

This review of UIFs identified important knowledge gaps. Some implicit hypotheses embedded in project designs, while intuitive and reasonable in principle, have little empirical basis. Project experiences have proven some hypotheses wrong, whereas others remain unexamined. Better knowledge in these areas would offer valuable information both for future IFI project design and for policymakers in developing countries. On the basis of this review, research is recommended in the following areas.

1. What is the experience of other donors with UIFs? How and why has it differed from that of the World Bank? How might products be differentiated or assistance in this area better coordinated?

2. What evidence is there of the impact of UIFs on overall infrastructure investment in small and medium cities? What are the other sources of funds available to them? Is UIF financing truly additive, and under what circumstances?

3. What have technical assistance components in UIF projects achieved—for municipalities, for intermediary institutions, and for the system of infrastructure finance? How well has technical assistance responded to the new demands arising from decentralization?

4. What types of incentives for better local financial management have been built into UIF programs, and what is the track record of these instruments (for example, performance grants, municipal contracts, interest rate subsidies)? In what circumstances has on-lending at market rates had the expected positive impact on financial discipline?

5. How has intergovernmental reform affected the level and quality of investments in municipalities? Which measures taken by government—financial incentives, regulation, direct administrative control, local electoral accountability, block grants, contracts, and the like—have been most effective in improving the quality and sustainability (maintenance) of investments undertaken by municipalities? Is it possible to begin to generalize as to when different strategies for maintenance and sustainability are most effective?

6. How has financial sector reform and the introduction of private market financing, along with UIF initiatives, affected such basic outcomes as (1) the types of local investments that can be most readily financed, (2) the quality of financial management and reporting, and (3) the vulnerability of local government capital spending to shifts in the credit market's pricing of risk?

CHAPTER 7

Conclusions

The demographic shift to smaller cities and towns in developing country cities predicted for the future—more than 750 million people from 2000 to 2015 alone—is dramatic and unprecedented. It will give rise to huge demands for new urban infrastructure services to be provided by local governments that now have limited capacity. **To maintain its reach and relevance, the World Bank must be able to provide decentralized urban infrastructure finance. This capacity is fundamental to scaling up beyond small pilot projects to programs improving urban services with a nationwide reach.**

Fortunately, the World Bank's long-standing experience with the UIF holds promise for meeting this operational challenge. This review sought to understand that experience to draw lessons for using this tool better, recognizing that the question is not whether the World Bank should support decentralized infrastructure finance, but how it could do so to greater effect. **A dramatic finding from this review, however, is that notwithstanding rapidly growing secondary cities, decentralization, and above-average performance in comparison to the World Bank portfolio and other lines of credit, the use of the urban infrastructures fund (UIFs) product is stagnating, and has been since the early 1990s. This trend should be reversed.**

One reason for this stagnation appears to be the shift in the World Bank's stance on lines of credit. Since the Levy report in 1989, the vision of intermediation for decentralized infrastructure finance has polarized. As the middle ground has given way, the scope for UIF operations declined more than was necessary. On the one hand, the Levy report and the ensuing Operational Directive (OD) and Operational Policy (OP) 8.30 argued that unprivileged market access must be the primary objective in a line of credit and placed the burden of proof on UIF lending operations to achieve this goal. Although this objective is unimpeachable in general terms, its universal applicability to urban local governments is questionable, as evidenced by the fairly common legal prohibition on local government borrowing.[1] At the opposite end of the spectrum, the community-driven poverty-oriented grant program, typically small and without institutional ambitions or substantive links to local government, became the instrument of choice when the market solution was not within immediate reach. With the "social fund," the World Bank quite rightly identified a need and developed a product to meet it. But combined with a strict interpretation of OD 8.30, this development made it easy to overlook opportunities to employ UIFs, providing finance combined with assistance for institutional development where market access was not imminent. If the World Bank is to use the UIF to its best potential, it must recognize the need to operate along the broad spectrum of intermediation models. Experiences show that projects deliberately adapted to the individualized needs of clients are more successful. Those that were adapted from other countries carelessly or whose project design was shoe-horned into broad corporate objectives faced problems.

Lessons from Experience

Do a few things well. The World Bank has developed workable models for a variety of needs and objectives, and the high average outcome ratings for UIFs attest to this. The many successful projects typically focused on one or two objectives and executed them simply. Less successful projects tried to combine all of them. The World Bank has supported projects that attracted private intermediaries to lend at their own risk for municipal infrastructure. It has developed programs that provide funding, mostly on a grant basis, to municipalities that have little borrowing capacity, and these programs have been tied, reasonably successfully, to performance improvements. Sometimes UIFs have been instrumental in achieving gradual improvements in the intergovernmental framework in which municipalities operate. The World Bank has supported agencies that have intervened effectively to mobilize rapidly previously underserved communities, offering them highly visible immediate relief. But the World Bank has also occasionally asked the intermediaries that it supports to mobilize funds in capital markets, while also lending larger and larger

---

[1]An interesting example of international financial institution support for such prohibitions is the Bosnia and Herzegovina case discussed in chapter 5. The International Monetary Fund (IMF) continues to oppose local government borrowing from commercial banks in spite of a successful project that mobilized funding from commercial banks at their own risk.

percentages to poor communities—in spite of weak evidence that such targeting reduces poverty at the household level and while also following procurement, fiduciary, and resettlement rules that competitors do not.

Assume that decentralization will proceed half as quickly as predicted, then halve that estimate again to come up with a credit market model and institutional development objectives. Some less successful projects picked an inferior design, typically relying heavily on local borrowing, based on the notion that a government declaration of decentralization or the expressed desire that municipalities fend for themselves is sufficient to make that model work. In some of the less successful projects, the existing administrative and financial wherewithal to borrow fell far short of what was needed to suit the more ambitious goals of the project. Optimism about the scope for improvement over the project period was excessive. In many of the better projects, the simple function of reaching out to local governments, helping them pick projects that met their needs and financial capacity, and locating the technical help to design a viable project was given considerable attention, and to good effect. Rather than promise more than a fund project could deliver in terms of intergovernmental reform, successful UIF projects, such as the Senegal Urban Development and Decentralization Project (UDDP), the Ghana Adaptable Program Loan (APL) urban project, and the first Financier de Desarrollo Territorial Sociedad Anonyma (FINDETER) project, seek incremental improvement of what is currently working in the system while building awareness of the next generation of issues to be tackled. It is notable, in this context, that many of the best performing projects are follow-on projects that build on contextual knowledge gained in earlier projects—knowledge critical to designing more ambitious UIFs. In addition, even within a country there is considerable diversity among local governments, and there is room for—arguably even a need for—a multiplicity of models. It is worth remembering that even in the United States in the 1980s, grants were thought necessary for cities providing services such as wastewater treatment. Bond banks were established to help small municipalities, while big cities readily tapped a flourishing municipal bond market.

Financial deregulation and decentralization have not made the UIF irrelevant; they have changed the way UIFs should be designed. The financial sectors in most of the World Bank's client countries have changed considerably in the past 20 years. Financial deregulation can bring in new players that may be interested in lending to local governments, provided this can be made a profitable business. Thus, whether or not to establish a dedicated intermediary with its own balance sheet or a facility that either lengthens maturities or mitigates risk is an important element of project design. Determining the pricing model becomes much more than just an exercise to assess whether rates are in line with the market. Building flexibility to respond to market movements and to reap the benefits of competition become much more important. Ignoring the implicit costs of working with a mode of delivering international financial institution assistance attuned to a rationed and controlled financial sector can substantially blunt the World Bank's impact. More pragmatic approaches to meeting the spirit of our safeguard rules are already being explored and need much more vigorous attention for UIFs.

Decentralization proceeds at a pace that has little to do with financial sector developments, so following the latest financial sector trends is far from enough to design a good municipal operation. The financial model the project seeks to use must be suited to the state of decentralization and the types of investment one wishes to support. No matter how dynamic the financial sector, it will not meet the investment needs of all local governments for all investments. Many important opportunities are missed by assuming that subsidies for urban investments are no longer needed because the financial sector is more flexible than it once was. Attention to improving the efficiency of investment subsidies for infrastructure services in small and medium towns has been sacrificed due to reluctance to countenance service subsidies in urban areas.

Be prepared for upside as well as downside risks. Some projects were less successful than they could have been because they did not offer the flexibility to respond well to positive developments. This is particularly important as financial markets deregulate and become more competitive. The Poland project was so concerned with strict enforcement of the eligibility criteria that it did not leave room for other institutions to opt in. The Tamil Nadu fund, concerned at appraisal with avoiding subsidized access to credit, was needlessly hampered by an interest rate formula that made it difficult to adapt when interest rates declined dramatically throughout India. Many of the projects offering loans to local governments suffered when alternative grant funds materialized unexpectedly. None of these problems is unmanageable if taken into account in project design.

Operational Issues for the Future

The recommendation to rebuild the UIF business line rests on a solid foundation of good project performance, as measured by the World Bank's independent evaluations. A number of models have emerged that have worked well in a variety of circumstances. Nonetheless, the lessons learned from experience also indicate a substantive agenda, not only for doing more of these projects, but also for doing them better and tailoring them to emerging needs. Some of the key operational issues to be addressed are

- creating an appropriate distance between a central government and its municipalities (sovereign guarantee and foreign exchange risk)
- responding to the diverse needs and capacities of the municipalities within a single country
- measuring results, including the quality of subprojects and the impact of UIF and other programs on access to funding and capital investment, with more rigor
- treating subsidies for urban infrastructure more flexibly and explicitly in UIFs
- designing funds that are user friendly to municipal borrowers and that make it easy for alternative financiers to "crowd in" with additional finance

Areas for Future Research and Analysis

In the course of the review, we identified important knowledge gaps. We recommend research should be undertaken in the following areas:

1. What is the experience of other donors in this same area?
2. What evidence do we have of the impact of UIFs on overall infrastructure investment in small and medium cities?
3. What have technical assistance components in UIF projects achieved—for municipalities, for intermediary institutions, and for the system of infrastructure finance? How well has technical assistance responded to the new demands arising from decentralization?
4. What types of incentives for better local financial management have been built into UIF programs, and what is the track record of these instruments (for example, performance grants, local government contracts, interest-rate subsidies)?
5. How has intergovernmental reform affected the level and quality of investments in municipalities?
6. How has financial sector reform affected the level and quality of investments in municipalities?

Methodology for Selecting and Identifying Urban Infrastructure Funds Financed by the World Bank

This data extraction has been achieved using the Enterprise Resource Planning integrated system SAP and its subcomponent Business Warehouse (BW). This system integrates all data and processes of the World Bank into a unified module. The purpose of the exercise was to identify all projects providing multisectoral urban infrastructure to more than one municipality or major city to support investment plans that were assessed and appraised by the project entity in country, not by the World Bank prior to appraisal. Because this represents a fairly broad range of projects managed by different groups, several criteria were applied to identify the group of urban infrastructure funds.

The projects' selection has been done using several filter criteria:

Criterion 1: Projects approved by the World Bank in FY1971–FY2006

- Objective: To learn from all World Bank project experience in retailing to municipalities. Given that the first project in urban development was implemented in 1971, project selection focused on FY1971–FY2006.
- At this stage, **8,206** projects were identified (see figure A1.1).

Figure A1.1. World Bank Project Approvals: FY1971–FY2006

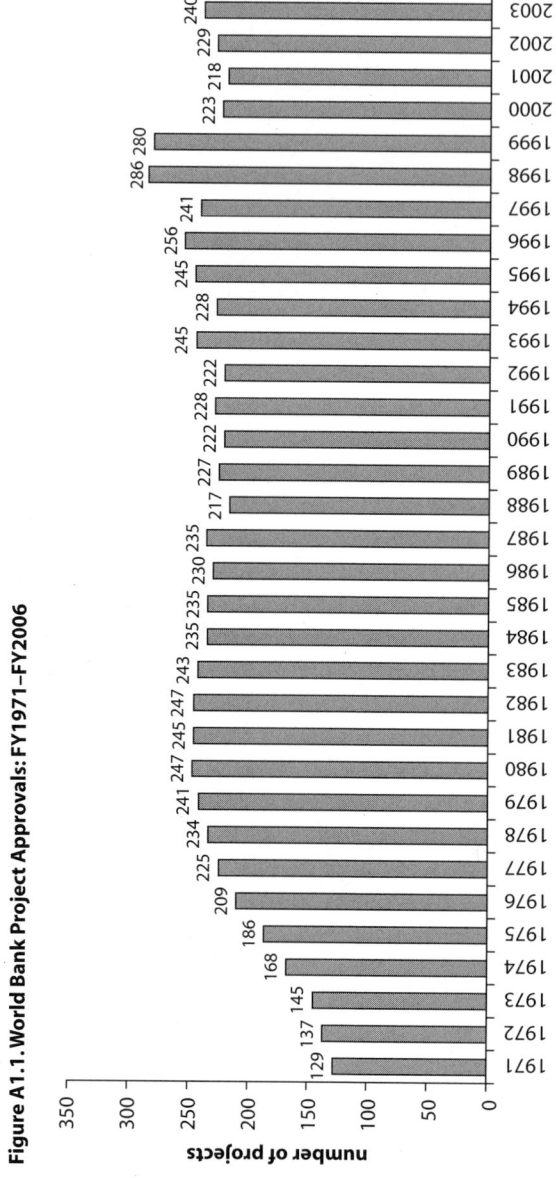

Source: Authors' calculations.

Criterion 2:

1) Projects approved in FY1986 or later

Selected projects will match the following criteria:
- Specific sectors: District Heating & Energy Efficiency Services (LA), Road & Highways (TA), General Transportation Sector (TZ), Sanitation (WA), Sewerage (WS), Solid Waste Management (WB), Water Supply (WC), General Water, Sanitation and Flood Protection Sector (WZ), Housing Construction (YC)
- Specific themes: Urban Development—Access to Urban Services for the Poor (71), Municipal Finance (72), Municipal Governance and Institution Building (73), Other Urban Development (74)
- Investment projects: Specific Investment Loan (SIL), Adaptable Program Loan (APL), Sector Investment and Maintenance Loan (SIM), Learning and Innovation Loan (LIL), Financial Intermediary Loan (FIL)

Excluded projects:
- Other sectors than those quoted
- Other themes than those quoted
- Emergency Recovery Loan (ERL), Technical Assistance Loan (TAL), Sector Adjustment Loan (SAD), Poverty Reduction Support Credit (PRSC), Structural Adjustment Loan (SAL), Special Structural Adjustment Loan (SSL)
- Emergency projects
- Utility projects

2) Projects approved before FY1986:

The World Bank database for projects prior to 1986 provides much less information on sectors and themes than for later projects. Accordingly, somewhat cruder filtering criteria had to be used to avoid reading hundreds of project documents. This means that some early UIF projects that were classified outside the Urban Development sector may have been excluded.

Selected projects will match the following criteria:
- Specific sectors: (Historic) Urban Development (UX)
- Investment projects: Specific Investment Loan (SIL), Sector Investment and Maintenance Loan (SIM), Financial Intermediary Loan (FIL)

- Excluded projects:
  - Other sectors than those quoted
  - Emergency Recovery Loan (ERL), Technical Assistance Loan (TAL), Sector Adjustment Loan (SAD), Structural Adjustment Loan (SAL), Special Structural Adjustment Loan (SSL)
  - Emergency projects
  - Utility projects

At this stage, **802** projects were identified meeting criteria 1 and 2.

Criterion 3: Selection of projects involving **multiple urban infrastructure services and multiple cities** and that were **decentralized finance projects.**

To achieve this goal, each of the **802** projects selected from the filters 1 and 2 were analyzed on the basis of information gathered from Project Appraisal Documents (PADs) and Staff Appraisal Report (SARs).

- In addition to using the World Bank's project database sectoral and thematic project coding, we also searched for specific keywords such as *multicity, line of credit, province, state,* and *region.*
- Multisector projects (that is, no more than 80 percent of the project is allocated to one subsector).
- Multicity projects

Following this methodology, we identified **104** projects meeting criteria 1, 2, and 3. **All those 104 projects constitute our large group of UIFs** for the statistical analysis in the stocktaking exercise. Table A1.1 summarizes the total number of projects financed by the World Bank by region. It also points out the total amount dedicated to these projects (amounts are given in constant 2006 dollars).

Table A1.1. UIF Projects by Region

Region	Number of projects	$ (constant 2006 million)
AFR	22	1,140
EAP	11	1,945
ECA	12	547
LAC	34	4,340
MNA	11	828
SAR	14	2,071
Total	**104**	**10,871**

Source: Authors' calculations.

For each of those 104 projects, we gathered the following information:

- Region: Africa (AFR) / East Asia and the Pacific (EAP) / Europe and Central Asia (ECA) / Latin America and the Caribbean (LCR) / Middle East and North Africa (MNA) / South Asia (SAR)
- Approval FY of the project and closing date
- Country
- Identification number of the project
- Project's name
- Sector Board: Economic Policy (EP) / Education (ED) / Energy and Mining (EMT) / Environment (ENV) / Financial Sector (FSE) / Global Information & Communications Technology (GIC) / Health, Nutrition and Population (HE) / Poverty Reduction (PO) / Public Sector Governance (PS) Private Sector Development (PSD) / Rural Sector (RDV) / Social Development (SDV) / Social Protection (SP) / Transport (TR) / Urban Development (UD) / Water Supply and Sanitation (WS)
- Project status: active / closed
- Borrower's name
- Implementing agency
- IBRD commitment amount
- IDA commitment amount
- Project's description
- Task Team Leader's name

APPENDIX 2

List of UIFs Reviewed

Region	Approval Fiscal Year	Country	Project ID	Project name	Loan/credit amount ($ millions)	Sector board	Project status (A: active, C: closed)
EAP	FY2006	Philippines	P064925	Support for Strategic Local Development and Investment	100	UD	A
LCR	FY2006	Brazil	P093787	Bahia State Integrated Project: Rural Poverty	54	RDV	A
LCR	FY2006	Haiti	P093640	Community Driven Development (CDD) Project / PRODEP	38	RDV	A
LCR	FY2006	Brazil	P052256	Rural Poverty Reduction Project— Minas Gerais	35	RDV	A
SAR	FY2006	Pakistan	P083929	Punjab Municipal Services Improvement Project	50	WSS	A
SAR	FY2006	India	P083780	Third Tamil Nadu Urban Development Project (TNUDP III)	300	UD	A
SAR	FY2006	India	P079675	Karnataka Municipal Reform Project	216	UD	A
AFR	FY2005	Chad	P066998	Local Development Program Support	23	SD	A
EAP	FY2005	Indonesia	P084583	Third Urban Poverty Project	138	UD	A
ECA	FY2005	Turkey	P081880	Turkey	275	UD	A
AFR	FY2004	Angola	P081558	Third Social Action Fund SIL (FY2004)	55	SP	A
ECA	FY2004	Kosovo	P079259	Community Development Fund 2	4	SP	A
SAR	FY2004	Pakistan	P082621	NWFP Community Infrastructure Project II (NWFP CIP2)	37	RDV	A
AFR	FY2003	Uganda	P077477	Second Local Government Development Project (FY2003)	125	PS	A

ECA	FY2003	Georgia	P077368	Municipal Development & Decentralization 2 Project	19	UD	A
ECA	FY2003	Bulgaria	P069532	Social Investment & Employment Promotion Project (SIEP)	50	SP	A
LAC	FY2003	Jamaica	P076837	National Community Development Project	15	UD	A
LAC	FY2003	Mexico	P060686	Municipal Development in Rural Areas	400	RDV	C
MNA	FY2003	Tunisia	P074398	Municipal Development Project (03)	78	UD	A
SAR	FY2003	Pakistan	P071454	AJK Community Infrastructure & Services Project	20	SDV	A
AFR	FY2002	Nigeria	P069901	Community-Based Urban Development Project	110	UD	A
EAP	FY2002	Indonesia	P072852	Second Urban Poverty Project (UPP2)	100	UD	A
LAC	FY2002	Ecuador	P039437	Poverty Reduction and Local Rural Development (PROLOCAL)	25	RDV	C
MNA	FY2002	Morocco	P073531	Support for the Social Development Agency Project	5	SP	A
AFR	FY2001	Burundi	P064961	Public Works & Employment Creation	40	UD	A
AFR	FY2001	Senegal	P041566	Social Development Fund	30	SP	C
ECA	FY2001	Bosnia and Herzegovina	P070995	Community Development Project	15	SP	A
LAC	FY2001	Nicaragua	P064906	Poverty Reduction & Local Development Project	60	SP	C
AFR	FY2000	Lesotho	P058050	Community Development Support Project	5	SP	C

(continued)

Region	Approval Fiscal Year	Country	Project ID	Project name	Loan/credit amount ($ millions)	Sector board	Project status (A: active, C: closed)
AFR	FY2000	Ghana	P050624	Urban Project (05)	11	UD	C
ECA	FY2000	Armenia	P057952	Social Investment Fund 2 (SIF2)	20	SP	C
MNA	FY2000	Lebanon	P050544	First Municipal Infrastructure Project	80	UD	A
AFR	FY1999	Gambia, The	P057997	Poverty Alleviation and Capacity Building Project	15	UD	C
AFR	FY1999	Gabon	P035626	Pilot Community Infrastructure Works and Capacity Building	5	UD	C
EAP	FY1999	Philippines	P048588	Local Government Finance & Development Project (LOGOFIND)	100	UD	A
ECA	FY1999	Bosnia and Herzegovina	P056192	Local Development Pilot Project	15	UD	C
ECA	FY1999	Albania	P051309	Community Works Project	9	SP	C
ECA	FY1999	Lithuania	P035802	Municipal Development Project	20	UD	C
LCR	FY1999	Nicaragua	P040197	Social Investment Fund Project (03)	45	SP	C
LCR	FY1999	Argentina	P006058	Fourth Social Protection Project	91	SP	C
SAR	FY1999	India	P050637	Tamil Nadu Urban Development Project (02)	105	UD	C
SAR	FY1999	Pakistan	P049791	Poverty Alleviation Fund	90	FSP	C
SAR	FY1999	Bangladesh	P041887	Municipal Services	139	UD	A
AFR	FY1998	Comoros	P044824	Social Fund Project	12	SP	C
AFR	FY1998	Senegal	P002365	Urban Development & Decentralization Program Project	75	UD	C

Region	FY	Country	Project ID	Project name	Number	Code	
ECA	FY1998	Georgia	P050910	Municipal Development and Decentralization Project	21	UD	C
ECA	FY1998	Poland	P035082	Municipal Finance Project	22	FS	C
LCR	FY1998	Colombia	P006861	Urban Infrastructure Services Development Loan	75	UD	C
MNA	FY1998	Jordan	P049581	Community Infrastructure Project	30	UD	C
MNA	FY1998	Morocco	P005523	Municipal Finance Project (02)	700	UD	C
AFR	FY1997	Madagascar	P048697	Regional Urban Works Project	35	UD	C
AFR	FY1997	Zimbabwe	P045029	Rural District Council Pilot Capital Development Project	12	UD	C
LCR	FY1997	Brazil	P043871	Rural Poverty Alleviation—Piaui	30	RDV	C
LCR	FY1997	Brazil	P042566	Rural Poverty Alleviation— Pernambuco	39	RDV	C
LCR	FY1997	Peru	P040125	Social Development and Compensation Fund (02)	150	SP	C
LCR	FY1997	Belize	P039292	Social Investment Fund	7	SP	C
LCR	FY1997	Jamaica	P039029	Social Investment Fund	20	SP	C
LCR	FY1997	Brazil	P038896	Rural Poverty Alleviation Rio Grande do Norte	24	RDV	C
MNA	FY1997	Tunisia	P046832	Municipal Development Project (02)	80	UD	C
AFR	FY1996	Eritrea	P039264	Community Development Fund Project	18	SP	C
AFR	FY1996	Mauritania	P034106	Urban Infrastructure and Pilot Decentralization	14	UD	C
ECA	FY1996	Latvia	P034584	Municipal Services Development Project	27	UD	C

(continued)

Region	Approval Fiscal Year	Country	Project ID	Project name	Loan/credit amount ($ millions)	Sector board	Project status (A: active, C: closed)
LCR	FY1996	Honduras	P037709	Social Investment Fund Project (03)	30	SP	C
LCR	FY1996	Bolivia	P006202	Rural Communities Development Project	15	RDV	C
MNA	FY1996	Yemen, Republic of	P043109	Public Works Project	25	UD	C
SAR	FY1996	Pakistan	P010478	NWFP–Community Infrastructure Project (CIP)	22	UD	C
LCR	FY1995	Mexico	P007702	Decentralization and Regional Development Project (02)	500	PSD	C
LCR	FY1995	Argentina	P006060	Municipal Development Project (02)	210	UD	C
LCR	FY1995	Argentina	P006018	Provincial Development Project (02)	225	PS	C
LCR	FY1994	Bolivia	P006190	Municipal Sector Development Project	42	UD	C
AFR	FY1993	Mauritania	P001870	Construction Capacity and Employment Project	12	SP	C
MNA	FY1993	Tunisia	P005687	Municipal Sector Investment Project	75	UD	C
MNA	FY1993	Morocco	P005517	Municipal Finance Project (01)	104	UD	C
EAP	FY1992	Philippines	P004592	Municipal Development Project (03)	68	UD	C
AFR	FY1991	São Tomé and Príncipe	P002548	Multisector Credit Project (02)	6	SP	C
AFR	FY1991	Niger	P001993	Public Works and Employment/ PACSA Project	20	SP	C
EAP	FY1991	Indonesia	P003943	East Java Bali Urban Development Project	180	UD	C
EAP	FY1991	China	P003520	Medium Sized Cities Development Project	168	UD	C

						TR	C
LCR	FY1991	Mexico	P007688	Decentralization and Regional Development Project	350	UD	C
LCR	FY1991	Colombia	P006852	Municipal Development Project	60	UD	C
AFR	FY1990	Côte d'Ivoire	P001156	Municipal Development Project	66	UD	C
EAP	FY1990	Philippines	P004573	Municipal Development Project (02)	40	UD	C
LCR	FY1990	Brazil	P006501	Municipal Development in the State of Rio Grande do Sul Project	100	UD	C
LCR	FY1989	Brazil	P006435	Parana Municipal Development Project	100	UD	C
SAR	FY1989	Nepal	P010326	Municipal Development and Earthquake Emergency Housing Reconstruction Project	42	UD	C
AFR	FY1988	Nigeria	P002099	Infrastructure Development Fund Project	70	UD	C
LCR	FY1988	Argentina	P005963	Municipal Development Project	120	UD	C
SAR	FY1988	India	P009872	Urban Development Project—Tamil Nadu	300	UD	C
ECA	FY1987	Turkey	P008970	Cukurova Urban Development Project	120	UD	C
MNA	FY1987	Tunisia	P005668	Urban Development Project (04)	30	UD	C
MNA	FY1987	Jordan	P005294	National Urban Development Program Project	26	UD	C
LCR	FY1986	Mexico	P007590	Municipal Strengthening Project	40	UD	C
LCR	FY1986	Brazil	P006398	Santa Catarina Small Towns Improvement Project	25	UD	C
LCR	FY1986	Brazil	P006367	Salvador Metropolitan Development Project	55	UD	C
SAR	FY1986	Sri Lanka	P010257	Municipal Management and Resource Mobilization Project	13	UD	C

(continued)

Region	Approval Fiscal Year	Country	Project ID	Project name	Loan/credit amount ($ millions)	Sector board	Project status (A: active, C: closed)
EAP	FY1985	Thailand	P004740	Secondary Cities Project	28	UD	C
LCR	FY1985	Honduras	P007364	Municipal Development Pilot Project	7	UD	C
EAP	FY1984	Philippines	P004501	Municipal Development Project	40	UD	C
LCR	FY1984	Brazil	P006343	Parana Market Towns Improvement Project	53	UD	C
AFR	FY1983	Kenya	P001288	Secondary Towns Project	29	UD	C
SAR	FY1983	India	P009809	Urban Development Project—Madhya Pradesh	24	UD	C
SAR	FY1983	India	P009808	Urban Development—Calcutta Project (03)	147	UD	C
LCR	FY1982	Nicaragua	P007765	Municipal Development Project	16	UD	C
EAP	FY1981	Indonesia	P003804	Urban Development Project (04)	43	UD	C
MNA	FY1980	Jordan	P005256	Municipal and Rural Development Bank	10	FS	C
EAP	FY1979	Indonesia	P003785	Urban Development Project (03)	54	UD	C
LCR	FY1979	Brazil	P006301	Medium-Sized Cities Project	70	UD	C

List of Currencies Available for Swaps from IBRD Loans as of January 3, 2008

IBRD Cross-Currency Swap Capabilities by Geographic Area

Area	Country	Currency
Asia and the Pacific	China	Chinese renminbi
	India	Indian rupee
	Indonesia	Indonesian rupiah
	Kazakhstan*	Kazakh tenge
	Malaysia	Malaysian ringgit
	Pakistan	Pakistan rupee
	Philippines	Philippine peso
	Korea, Rep. of	Korean won
	Thailand	Thai baht
Europe	Bulgaria	Bulgarian lev
	Croatia	Croatian kuna
	Hungary	Hungarian forint
	Latvia*	Latvia lats
	Poland	Polish zloty
	Romania	Romanian leu
	Russian Fed.	Russian ruble
	Serbia*	Serbian dinar
	Slovakia	Slovak koruna
	Turkey	Turkish lira
	Ukraine*	Ukraine hryvnia
Latin America	Argentina	Argentinian peso
	Brazil	Brazilian real
	Chile	Chilean peso
	Colombia	Colombian peso
	Costa Rica*	Costa Rican colón
	Dominican Rep.*	Dominican peso
	Guatemala*	Guatemalan quetzal
	Mexico	Mexican peso
	Panama*	Panamanian balboa
	Paraguay*	Paraguayan guaraní
	Peru	Peruvian new sol
	Uruguay*	Uruguayan peso
Middle East and Africa	Algeria*	Algerian dinar
	Botswana	Botswanan pula
	Egypt, Arab Rep. of	Egyptian pound
	Jordan*	Jordanian dinar
	Mauritius*	Mauritian rupee
	Morocco	Moroccan dirham
	Namibia	Namibian dollar
	Nigeria	Nigerian naira
	South Africa	South Africa rand
	Tunisia	Tunisian dinar

*Poor liquidity. Transaction volume less than $10 million equivalent. Larger volumes can be considered on a case-by-case basis. Swap tenors might also be subject to restrictions.
*As of January 3, 2008.

References

Publications

Agence Française de Développement. 2005. *Financer les investissements des villes des pays en développement*. Notes et documents N°24. Paris: Agence Française de Développement.

Banerjee, Abhijit. 2007. "Inside the Machine." In *Making Aid Work*, ed. Abhijit Banerjee. Boston: Boston Review/MIT Press.

Boskin, Michael J., Marc S. Robinson, and Alan M. Huber. 1987. "Government Saving, Capital Formation and Wealth in the United States, 1947–1985." Working Paper No. 2352, National Bureau of Economic Research, Cambridge, MA. August.

Buckley, Robert, and Jerry Kalarickal. 2006. *Thirty Years of World Bank Shelter Lending: What Have We Learned?* World Bank Directions in Development Series. Washington, DC: World Bank.

Davey, Kenneth. 1988. *Municipal Development Funds and Intermediaries*. Policy, Planning, and Research Department Working Paper No. 32, World Bank, Washington, DC.

El Daher, Samir. 2001. "The Building Blocks of a Sound Local Government Finance System." *Infrastructure Notes*, Urban No. FM-8e, World Bank, Washington, DC.

———. 2000. "Specialized Financial Intermediaries for Local Governments: A Market-Based Tool for Local Infrastructure Finance." *Infrastructure Notes*, Urban No. FM-8d, World Bank, Washington, DC.

Ferguson, Bruce. 1993. "The Design of Municipal Development Funds." *Review of Urban and Regional Development Studies* 5 (2): 154–73.

Infrastructure Vice Presidency, World Bank. 2005. *Infrastructure and the World Bank: A Progress Report*. Washington, DC: World Bank. September.

Lee, Kyu Sik. 1999. "Municipal Development Projects: Building Institutions and Financing Local Development." Précis No. 178, World Bank Operations Evaluation Department, Washington, DC.

National Research Council. 2003. *Cities Transformed: Demographic Change and Its Implications for the Developing World*. Washington, DC: National Academies Press.

OED (World Bank Operations Evaluation Department). 2005a. *The Effectiveness of World Bank Support for Community-Driven Development*. Washington, DC: World Bank. January.

————. 2005b. "Review of Bank Lending for Lines of Credit." Report No. 31131, World Bank, Washington, DC. January.

————. 2002. *Social Funds: Assessing Effectiveness*. Washington, DC: World Bank.

————. 1999. "Municipal Development Projects: Financing Local Development and Building Institutions." Précis No. 178, World Bank Operations Evaluation Department, Washington, DC.

Paulais, Thierry. 2006. "Le financement du développement urbain dans les pays émergents: Des besoins et des paradoxes." *Revue d'économie financière* 86: 309–30.

Petersen, John. 2004. *Decentralized Credit Financing of Infrastructure in Developing Countries: An Assessment of Techniques*. Fairfax, VA: George Mason University. August.

Peterson, George. 2000. *Building Local Credit Systems*. World Bank Municipal Finance Background Series No. 3. Washington, DC: World Bank. April.

————. 1998. "Measuring Local Government Credit Risk and Improving Credit-Worthiness." World Bank, Washington, DC, March.

————. 1996. "Using Municipal Development Funds to Build Municipal Credit Markets." World Bank, Washington, DC, August.

United Nations, Economic and Social Affairs Department, Population Division. 2006. *World Urbanization Prospects: The 2005 Revision*. Geneva: United Nations.

Zinnes, Clifford S. 2008. *Tournament Approaches to Public Policy Implementation: Current Practice and Scope for Future Applications*. Washington, DC: Wolfensohn Center for Development, The Brookings Institution.

Presentations

Annez, Patricia. 2006. "Municipal Finance Learning Event: The Role and Evolution of Municipal Funds." Presented at Urban Learning Week, World Bank, Washington, DC, March 22–23.

Aweida, Ahmed. 2007. "Lessons Learned from World Bank Support of Local Government and Decentralization." Presented at World Bank Municipal Finance Thematic Group Brown Bag Lunch, Washington, DC, May 23.

Abousleiman, Issam. 2007. "How IBRD Loans and Banking Products Can Reduce the Risk of Lending to Local Governments." Presented at World Bank Municipal Finance Thematic Group Brown Bag Lunch, Washington, DC, February 28.

Kesavan, Raghu. 2006. "Operational Issues in Designing Municipal Fund Interventions." Presented at Urban Learning Week, World Bank, Washington, DC, March 22–23.

Khan, Kamran. 2005. "Towards a Framework for Involving Financial Intermediaries in Municipal Finance Projects." Presented at Urban Learning Week, World Bank, Washington, DC, March 22–23.

Peterson, George. 2006. "Overview of International Experience with Municipal Funds." Presented at Urban Learning Week, World Bank, Washington, DC, March 22–23.

World Bank Guidelines

World Bank.1998. "Financial Intermediary Lending." *Bank Procedures*, BP8.30, and *Operational Policies*, OP8.30.

World Bank. 1989. *Report on the Task Force on Financial Sector Operations.* R98-163. Washington, DC: World Bank. August 1.

Web Sites

United Cities and Local Governments. http://www.cities-localgovernments.org/uclg/.

Index

Boxes, figures, notes, and tables are indicated by b, f, n, and t respectively.

Adamawa (Nigeria), 32
Adaptable Program Loan (Ghana APL), 65
Africa, 7*t*, 9, 26, 36, 38, 39
  See also Sub-Saharan Africa; *individual countries*
Agence d'Exécution de Travaux d'Intérêt Public (AGETIP), 26, 39
aggregate financing, 56–57
all-lending model, 31, 34, 36
  See also on-lending
Austria, 50

Bangladesh, 37
Bank Policy (BP) 8.30, 25
banks. *See* commercial banks
Bombay. *See* Mumbai (India)
borrowing, 32, 34–35
  See also loans
Bosnia and Herzegovina, 47, 50, 64*n*1
Brazil, 31*n*1
Business Warehouse (BW), 69

Caisse des Prêts et de Soutien aux Collectivités Local (CPSCL), 45
Chongqing (China), xx, 2
city size, 2, 4, 4*f*, 5*f*
Columbia, 46–47
commercial banks, xxiii, 46–50, 58*b*–59*b*, 64*n*1
"community-driven development," 38
Côte d'Ivoire Municipal Fund Development Project, 34, 35
Credit Local de France (CLF), 24*b*, 43, 44
credit market model, xxi, 22–25, 29, 36–37, 53, 65
credit risks, 23, 24*b*, 35, 47, 49
  See also foreign exchange risks
currencies, 83–84
Czech Republic, 50, 57, 58*b*–59*b*

decentralization
  country systems and, 61
  credit risk and, 49
  fiscal discipline and, 52
  in India, 36
  intermediation models and, 23
  local infrastructure investment and, 43

decentralization—*continued*
  outcomes of, 15, 46
  pace of, xxii, xxiv, 12, 24*b*, 29, 65, 66
  role of, 5–6
  UIF design and, xxiii
democratization, x, 51, 61
demographics, xx–xxi, 2–5, 63
deregulation, xxiii, 65–66
Development Policy Loans (DPLs), 4, 54
directed credit, xxiv, 6, 15, 19, 23, 24*b*, 34

economic rates of return (ERRs), 55*n*3,
  55–56
Enterprise Resource Planning, 69
European Investment Bank (EIB), 48
European Union (EU), 48

financial intermediation model, 26–27,
  27*t*, 29, 31–32, 33*t*
Financial Sector (FS), 9
financial sector liberalization, xxiii, 6, 15,
  53, 61
Financiera de Desarrollo Territorial
  Sociedad Anonyma (FINDETER),
  46–47, 65
financing. *See* aggregate financing;
  poverty-oriented grant financing
Fonds d'Equipement Communal (FEC),
  43–44, 53
foreign exchange risks, 49–50, 52–53, 67
  See also credit risks
France, 6, 23, 24*b*
future operational issues, xxv, 66–67
future research and analysis, 67
future work agenda, 51–62
  central government and municipalities,
    xxv, 52–53, 67
  future research and analysis, xxvi, 62,
    67
  measuring results, xxv, 54–56, 67
  needs and capacities of municipalities,
    xxv, 53–54, 67
  operational challenges, 52–61
  subsidies for UIFs, xxv, 57, 60, 67
  user friendly funds, xxv, 60–61, 67

Georgia (country), 41–42
Ghana, 65
grants
  See also loans; poverty-oriented grant
    financing; subsidies
  loans vs., 27*f*, 34–35, 57, 60, 66

models for, 27
municipal, 37–43, 40*t*
performance, 42–43
questionnaire responses and, 55*n*4
social funds and, xxiv
UIF projects, xxii, 14*f*, 15
gross domestic product (GDP), 4, 7*n*7, 41
growth. *See* population growth

Implementation Completion Reports
  (ICRs), 39, 44, 55, 56*n*6
Independent Evaluation Group (IEG), 17,
  18*f*, 51
India, xxii, 36–37, 45, 66
Infrastructure Action Plan (IAP), xxi, 12,
  29
Infrastructure Sectors, 12, 12*f*, 29
initial public offering (IPO), 44
Inter-American Development Bank
  (IADB), 47
intermediation strategies, 21–29
  credit market model and, xxi, 22–25,
    29
  on-lending, 22–25
  poverty-oriented grant financing,
    25–29, 27*t*
International Bank for Reconstruction and
  Development (IBRD), xxi, 13,
  52–53, 83–84
International Development Association
  (IDA), xxi, 13
International Finance Corporation (IFC),
  13*n*1, 53
international financial institutions (IFIs)
  decentralization and, 5–6
  directed credit and, 15
  financial sector liberalization and, 61
  FINDETER support through, 47
  grants through, 60
  institutional arrangements of, 51
  level of involvement, xx, 4, 57
  sovereign guarantees and, 53
International Monetary Fund (IMF), 47,
  64*n*1

Latin America and the Caribbean Region
  (LAC), 9, 31, 38
less developed countries (LDCs), 1, 2
  See also middle-income countries
    (MICs); *individual countries*
lessons from experience, xxi–xxv, 64–66
Levy report (World Bank), 13, 25, 55, 63

liberalization. *See* financial sector
liberalization
lines of credit (LOC)
performance of, xx, 17
private sector finance and, 25
problems with, 15, 18–19
stagnation and, 13, 63–64
in Sub-Saharan Africa, 31–35, 37
TNUDF and, 37
Lithuania, 48–49
loans
See also borrowing; grants
grants vs., 27f, 34, 57, 60, 66
MUFIS and, 58b–59b
repayment of, 19, 20f, 26, 32, 33t, 35,
42
Local Government Loans Authority
(Kenya), 35

Madras (India), 36
market-oriented reform, 23, 24b
mega-cities, 4, 5f
middle-income countries (MICs), xxi, 13,
46, 49
See also less developed countries
(LDCs); *individual countries*
Morocco, xxii, 43–45, 53
Multilateral Investment Guarantee
Agency (MIGA), 13n1
Mumbai (India), xx, 2
Municipal Adjustment Plan (MAP), 39, 41
municipal credit, 28, 28f, 46–49
municipal development funds (MDFs),
xixn1, xxiii, 1n2, 6, 29, 34, 48–49
Municipal Infrastructure Finance
Company (MUFIS), 58b–59b

Nigeria, 11, 32, 35
nongovernmental organizations (NGOs),
xixn1, 1n2, 26

objectives of UIFs, 1–8
See also urban infrastructure funds
decentralization and, 5–6
demographics and, xx–xxi, 2–5
financial liberalization and, 6
growth rates, 4, 4f
low- and middle income vs. high-
income countries, 2, 3f
population growth by city size, 2, 4f
review of experience, 7–8
urban vs. rural population growth, 2, 3f

on-lending, xxii–xxiii, 18, 22–25, 33t, 37,
48, 56n5, 58b
See also all-lending model
OP. *See* Operational Policy
Operational Directive (OD) 8.30, 13, 15,
25, 36, 63–64
Operational Policy (OP) 8.30, 25, 63–64
Operations Evaluation Department
(OED), 15, 17–18, 26
outcome ratings, 17, 18f

Pakistan, 37, 54
performance targets, 39
Peru Social Fund, 25–26
Poland, 47–48, 49–50, 66
population growth, 2, 3f, 4, 4f
poverty-oriented grant financing, xxi–xxii,
25–29, 27f, 27t, 64
See also grants
Prague (Czech Republic), 59b
private market access. *See* credit market
model
Private Sector Development (PSD), 9
Project Appraisal Documents (PADs),
44, 72
project design, 31–50
commercial banks and, 46–50
credit model adaptation, 36–37
credit risk and, 49
foreign exchange risk and, 49–50
line of credit model, 31–35
municipal credit and, 46–49, 50
municipal grants and, 37–43, 40t
municipal infrastructure investment
support, 43–46
price model determination for, 66
social funds and, 37–39
in South Asia, 36–37
in Sub-Saharan Africa, 31–35, 33t
Public-Private Partnership (PPP), 54
Punjab (Pakistan), 54

reform. *See* market-oriented reform
repayment rates and repayment capacity,
19, 20f, 26, 32, 33t, 35, 42
risk. *See* credit risks; foreign exchange risks
Rose Revolution (Georgia), 42
Rural Development (RDV), 9–10, 10f, 17,
25, 27, 57

São Paulo (Brazil), xx, 2
"second window" problem, 35

sector boards, 9, 10*f*, 10–11, 11*f*, 18*f*, 27*f*,
    28*f*
    See also individual sector boards, e.g.
        Urban Development
Senegal, 39, 40*t*, 41, 65
74th Constitutional Amendment Act
    (India), 36
Social Development (SDV), 9–10
social funds, xxiii–xxiv, xxiv, 25–26, 29,
    37–39, 55, 64
Social Protection (SP), 9, 10*f*, 17, 25, 27,
    57
South Africa, 32
South Asia, 36–37
    See also individual countries
sovereign guarantees, 53, 67
SP. *See* Social Protection
Staff Appraisal Reports (SARs), 72
subproject selections, 54–56, 67
Sub-Saharan Africa, xxii, 31–35, 33*t*, 37
    See also Africa; *individual countries*
subsidies, xxiv, xxv, 57, 60, 66, 67
    See also grants
swaps, 83–84

Tamil Nadu, 36–37, 45, 66
Tamil Nadu Urban Development Fund
    (TNUDF), 36–37, 45
Tarala (Nigeria), 32
Tunisia, xxii, 6, 45

United States, 4, 23, 65
United States Agency for International
    Development (USAID), 34, 57,
    58*b*, 59*b*
Urban Decentralization and Investment
    Project (Senegal), 39
Urban Development and Decentralization
    Project (Senegal UDDP), 65
Urban Development (UD)
    financial intermediation model and,
        26–28
    municipal credit markets and, 29
    performance of, 12–13, 17–18

projects under, 7, 9–10, 10*f*, 11*f*
share of UIFs in portfolio, xxi
social funds and, 38–39
subsidies through, 57
urban infrastructure funds (UIFs), 9–15
    See also objectives of UIFs
    commitments by country, 9, 10*f*
    design of, 21–29
    disbursements, 19, 19*f*
    grant projects, 14*f*, 15
    key characteristics of, 1–2
    lending, 11*f*, 11–15, 14*f*
    list of reviewed, 75–82
    objectives of, 1–8
    performance of, 17–20, 18*f*, 19*f*
    project size, 12–13, 13*f*
    by region, 7, 7*t*
    repayment rates, 19, 20*f*
    by sector boards, 9, 10*f*, 10–11, 11*f*, 18*f*
    selection and identification, 7, 7*n*6,
        69–73
USAID (United States Agency for
    International Development), 34

Water Supply and Sanitation (WSS), 9
World Bank
    decentralization and, 5–6
    Development Policy Loans (DLPs), 4
    directed credit and, 15
    foreign current risks, 50
    intermediation strategies, 22, 23
    line of credit operations and, 13, 17
    municipal credit and, 46–49
    municipal infrastructure investment
        support and, 43–46
    projects approvals, 7–8, 69, 70*f*, 71–73,
        72*t*
    projects in Georgia, 41–42
    projects in India, 36–37, 45
    projects in Tunisia, 45
    Second Municipal Finance Project, 44
    sovereign guarantees and, 53

Zimbabwe, 32